First World War

and Army of Occupation

War Diary

France, Belgium and Germany

61 DIVISION
183 Infantry Brigade,
Brigade Machine Gun Company
17 June 1916 - 23 June 1916

WO95/3062/3

The Naval & Military Press Ltd
www.nmarchive.com
Published in association with The National Archives

Published by

The Naval & Military Press Ltd

Unit 10 Ridgewood Industrial Park,

Uckfield, East Sussex,

TN22 5QE England

Tel: +44 (0) 1825 749494

www.naval-military-press.com

www.nmarchive.com

This diary has been reprinted in facsimile from the original. Any imperfections are inevitably reproduced and the quality may fall short of modern type and cartographic standards.

Contents

Document type	Place/Title	Date From	Date To
War Diary	Ford Ham	25/06/1916	25/06/1916
War Diary	In The Field	27/06/1916	27/06/1916
War Diary	In The Field (Heim Chapel)	28/06/1916	30/06/1916
Heading	War Diary of 183rd Machine Gun Coy from 1st July-31st July 1916 Vol		
War Diary	Lestrem	01/07/1916	02/07/1916
War Diary	In The Field	03/07/1916	31/07/1916
Heading	183rd Inf Bde War Diary of 183 Machine Gun Coy Aug 1st-31st 1916 Vol 3		
War Diary	In The Field	01/08/1916	31/08/1916
Heading	183rd Infantry Brigade War Diary Of 183rd Machine Gun Company For September 1916 Vol 4		
War Diary	In The Field	01/09/1916	30/09/1916
Heading	183 Inf. Bde. 183rd Bde M.G. Coy War Diary For October 1916		
War Diary	In The Field	01/10/1916	31/10/1916
Heading	War Diary of 183 Machine Gun Company For November 1916		
War Diary	In The Field	01/11/1916	30/11/1916
Heading	War Diary 183 M.G.Coy. December 1916 Vol 7		
War Diary	In The Field	01/12/1916	31/12/1916
Heading	War Diary of 183rd Machine Gun Company for January 1917 Vol 8		
War Diary	In The Field	01/01/1917	13/01/1917
War Diary	Hedeauville	14/01/1917	15/01/1917
War Diary	Beauquesne	16/01/1917	16/01/1917
War Diary	Grimont	17/01/1917	17/01/1917
War Diary	Conteville	18/01/1917	18/01/1917
War Diary	Argenvillers	19/01/1917	31/01/1917
Heading	February 1917 War Diary of 183 Machine Gun Company Vol 9		
War Diary	Argenvillers	01/02/1917	05/02/1917
War Diary	St Firmin	06/02/1917	11/02/1917
War Diary	Ergnies	12/02/1917	15/02/1917
War Diary	Framerville	16/02/1917	16/02/1917
War Diary	Trenches	17/02/1917	21/02/1917
War Diary	Trenches Kratz Sous. Sector	22/02/1917	25/02/1917
War Diary	Harbonniers	26/02/1917	28/02/1917
Heading	March 1917 War Diary Of 183 Machine Gun Coy Vol 10		
War Diary	Harbonnieres	01/03/1917	07/03/1917
War Diary	Trenches	08/03/1917	23/03/1917
War Diary	In The Field	24/03/1917	31/03/1917
Heading	April 1917 War Diary Of 183 Machine Gun Coy Vol XI		
War Diary	In The Field	01/04/1917	30/04/1917
Heading	May 1917 War Diary of 183rd Machine Gun Coy Vol 12		
War Diary	In The Field	01/05/1917	31/05/1917

Heading	June 1917 War Diary Of 183rd Machine Gun Coy Vol 13		
War Diary	Tilloy	01/06/1917	10/06/1917
War Diary	Simencourt	11/06/1917	21/06/1917
War Diary	Neulette	22/06/1917	30/06/1917
Heading	183 Machine Gun Coy War Diary Vol 14 July 1917		
War Diary	Neulette	01/07/1917	24/07/1917
War Diary	Ecoivres Petit Hounin	25/07/1917	25/07/1917
War Diary	Petit Hounin	26/07/1917	31/07/1917
Heading	August 1917 War Diary Of 183 Machine Gun Coy Vol 15		
War Diary	Zeggers Cappel. Area	01/08/1917	19/08/1917
War Diary	Wieltje	20/08/1917	29/08/1917
War Diary	Vlamertinge	30/08/1917	31/08/1917
Heading	Sep 1917 War Diary Of 183rd Machine Gun Coy Vol 16		
War Diary	Vlamertinghe N Ypres	01/09/1917	07/09/1917
War Diary	Weiltje	07/09/1917	17/09/1917
War Diary	Watou	18/09/1917	18/09/1917
War Diary	Wormhoudt	19/09/1917	19/09/1917
War Diary	Simencourt	20/09/1917	27/09/1917
War Diary	Fampoux	28/09/1917	30/09/1917
Heading	October 1917 War Diary Of 183rd Machine Gun Coy Vol 17		
War Diary	Green Land Hill	01/10/1917	04/10/1917
War Diary	St Nicholas	05/10/1917	14/10/1917
War Diary	Fampoux	15/10/1917	31/10/1917
Miscellaneous	Headquarters, 61st. Division	26/12/1917	26/12/1917
Miscellaneous	To Hqrs (Ream 183 Infantry Brigade From OC 183 ON GL (Res)	20/12/1917	20/12/1917
War Diary	Fampoux	01/11/1917	07/11/1917
War Diary	Arras	08/11/1917	20/11/1917
War Diary	Greenland Hill	21/11/1917	30/11/1917
Heading	December 1917 War Diary Of 183rd Machine Gun Coy Vol 19		
War Diary	Metz	01/12/1917	31/12/1917
Heading	January 1918 War Diary Of 183rd Machine Gun Coy Vol 20		
War Diary	Marcelcave Rea Sheet Amiens	01/01/1918	06/01/1918
War Diary	Roiglise Ref Sheet 66D 1:40.000	07/01/1918	08/01/1918
War Diary	Falvy Ref. Sheet 66 D.	09/01/1918	09/01/1918
War Diary	Ref. Sheet 66 D 1,40.000 Falvy	10/01/1918	13/01/1918
War Diary	Ref Sheet 62C S.E. 1,20,000	14/01/1918	18/01/1918
War Diary	Ref Sheet 62 C S E 1,20,000 S.10.c.30 95	18/01/1918	23/01/1918
War Diary	S.10.C. 30.95	24/01/1918	30/01/1918
War Diary	Ref Sheet 23 S 10. C.30.95	30/01/1918	31/01/1918
Miscellaneous	183 Machine Gun Company Training Programme From 16th January 1918 Appendix I		
Miscellaneous	183 Machine Gun Company Training Programme From January 2nd 1915 Appendix II		
War Diary	Ref Sheet 62 B S.W. 1,20,000 Sioc 30.95	01/02/1918	03/02/1918
War Diary	Ref Sheet France St Quentin 1.100.000 300x Sof X In Vaux	03/02/1918	10/02/1918
War Diary	Vaux Ref Sheet 62 B SW 1,20.0000 M27.a 68 Fresnoy	10/02/1918	15/02/1918
War Diary	Fresnoy	16/02/1918	27/02/1918
War Diary	Vaux	28/02/1918	28/02/1918

Heading	WO95/3062 (3)		
Heading	183rd Machine Gun Coy Jun 1916-Feb 1918		
War Diary	Le Havre	17/06/1916	19/06/1916
War Diary	C Gorgue	19/06/1916	20/06/1916
War Diary	Lestrem	21/06/1916	23/06/1916

Instructions regarding War Diaries and Intelligence Summaries are contained in F. S. Regs., Part II. and the Staff Manual respectively. Title Pages will be prepared in manuscript.

WAR DIARY
or
~~INTELLIGENCE SUMMARY~~

(Erase heading not required.)

183 M. G. Coy.

Army Form C. 2118.

Place	Date	Hour	Summary of Events and Information	Remarks and references to Appendices
[illegible]	25.6.16		Inspection of positions by O.C. & 2nd in Com. & arrangements made for 3 & 4 sections to move up for instruction, also for indirect fire by 1 & 2 sections in conjunction with the operation.	CW
		11.15 pm	Our guns operating with 56 Btn. searched enemy Communications in ~~on~~ the flanks of the Bois du Biez, in conjunction with artillery bombardment. A few minutes after, the front line guns traversed the enemy front line parapet. This	CW
		12.45 am	was repeated at 11.45 pm. The enemy reply was late & therefore ineffective, guns returning without casualties.	CW
	26.6.16		During the day A. 3 & 4 sections relieved 105 M. G. Coy in the front & 2nd line with 8 guns, & the reserve posts in the 3rd line were taken over by 2 section during the night, with 4 guns, the remaining 4 guns of No. 1 section remaining at Hqrs. near "Green Barn" [illegible], taken over during the early hours of	CW
[illegible]	27.6.16		27th. The day was quiet & was spent in repairing damage to parapets &c. caused by heavy bombardment of our front line in the early hours of the previous morning. ~~[illegible]~~ The front line guns dispersed enemy working parties during the night. Our Lozy positions came under hostile M.G. & gun fire & shrapnel ~~[illegible]~~ & our guns here did not fire.	CW

CWalker

Army Form C. 2118.

WAR DIARY
or
~~INTELLIGENCE SUMMARY~~
(Erase heading not required.)

183 R. E. Coy.

Instructions regarding War Diaries and Intelligence Summaries are contained in F. S. Regs., Part II. and the Staff Manual respectively. Title Pages will be prepared in manuscript.

Place	Date	Hour	Summary of Events and Information	Remarks and references to Appendices
In the field (Neuve Chapelle)	28.6.16		Our front line guns fired with good effect on enemy working parties in the early hours of the morning. Repairs & draining work was carried out. Enemy communications in & on the flanks of the Bois du Biez were again searched with indirect fire & also the La Bassée road behind their front line. It had been observed that the enemy, who apparently knew the hour of "stand down", used to come out after daybreak & carry out work without molestation. Our gunners therefore "stand to" for another hour & the enemy's former practice is not now carried out. Working parties in the daylight were dispersed very effectively on this morning & sentries have received special orders to look out for this sort of thing. Hdqrs. came under shrapnel fire directed on the road to our flank.	CW
"	29.6.16		Indirect fire was again applied as on yesterday evening, & traversing fire by our front line guns effectively prevented the enemy repairing gaps in their wire. One party making the attempt later in the morning were dispersed in great haste.	CW
"	30.6.16		The indirect fire was applied in combination with other operations on our right & a heavy bombardment by artillery. We suffered 2 casualties (wounded) during this bombardment.	CW

CWaller

2449 Wt. W14957/M90 750,000 1/16 J.B.C. & A. Forms/C.2118/12.

Instructions regarding War Diaries and Intelligence Summaries are contained in F. S. Regs., Part II. and the Staff Manual respectively. Title Pages will be prepared in manuscript.

WAR DIARY
or
~~INTELLIGENCE~~ SUMMARY
(Erase heading not required.)

183 R. E. Coy. Army Form C. 2118.

Place	Date	Hour	Summary of Events and Information	Remarks and references to Appendices
In the field & Bois Grenier [?] Lestrem	30.6.16		182 R. E. Coy. relieved us. The day was very quiet. Moved into billets at Lestrem at about 11.0 pm.	CW

C. W. Walker [?]
Commdg 183 R E Co.

2449 Wt. W14957/M90 750,000 1/16 J.B.C. & A. Forms/C.2118/12.

61

Vol ~~III~~ 2

CONFIDENTIAL

WAR DIARY.

— of —

183rd. MACHINE GUN COY.

from 1st July - 31st July 1916.

Vol: 3

Instructions regarding War Diaries and Intelligence Summaries are contained in F. S. Regs., Part II. and the Staff Manual respectively. Title Pages will be prepared in manuscript.

WAR DIARY
or
~~INTELLIGENCE~~ SUMMARY
(Erase heading not required.)

183 M. G. Coy.

Army Form C. 2118.

Place	Date	Hour	Summary of Events and Information	Remarks and references to Appendices
Lëtten	1.7.16		Morning kit inspection, limber inspection & cleaning.	CW
			Afternoon rest – deficiencies indented for.	CW.
"	2.7.16		Inspection of iron rations & gas helmets. Preparations for a move in the morning.	CW.
In the field	3.7.16	6 a.m.	Moved to Laventie & relieved 184 M. G. Coy. in the "Fauquissart–Area". Work was carried on during the spare hours of today in improving emplacements for indirect fire.	CW.
		11.30 pm	Indirect fire was applied from Jock's Lodge against enemy communication [illegible] at on the vicinity of points N 8 d. 5.2 & N. 14 b. 3.1. These positions were fired at intermittently till daylight. The enemy replied briskly & from the accuracy of his fire the fire position was known to him & registered. The exact positions of guns had to be changed.	CW.
			Front line guns fired during the night on gaps in the enemy wire and a breach in his parapet at N 19 C 2.8. These gaps were kept open. Three enemy rifle grenades & a trench mortar chased our gun in the vicinity of Sally post ½ but were unable to silence it.	CW.
			Enemy artillery activity against Fauquissart & Elbow posts, points to his accurate knowledge of these positions.	CW
"	4.7.16		The enemy's practice of attempting to working operations during the early hours of daylight was again stopped in the bud on this front.	CW
			During the day sections worked on improvements to their positions.	CW
		10.15	Fire by front line guns on enemy's parapet in ~~conn~~ connection with Brigade raiding operations. In connection with the same operations 3 guns applied indirect fire to enemy communications on the flanks of the 2 points raided & 2 guns kept up a barrage behind these points. Fire is believed to have been very effective.	CW CW.

Instructions regarding War Diaries and Intelligence Summaries are contained in F. S. Regs., Part II. and the Staff Manual respectively. Title Pages will be prepared in manuscript.

WAR DIARY
or
~~INTELLIGENCE SUMMARY~~
(Erase heading not required.)

183 M. G. Coy.

Army Form C. 2118.

Place	Date	Hour	Summary of Events and Information	Remarks and references to Appendices
In the field	4.7.16		During these operations Fauquissart & Masselot House posts were intensely bombarded.	CWW
	5.7.16		Day was quiet & spent at work on defences.	
"			At 10.30 p.m. one gun applied indirect fire on point N19a 3½ 3 & communication in rear, but was obliged to evacuate its position under accurate artillery & m.g. fire. 2nd Lt. J. C. Paton received 3 m.g. bullets through the fleshy part of his leg & thigh during this period. He has done excellent work with No 4 Section.	CWW CWW
			Front line guns (4) fired intermittently through the night at enemy's parapet & gaps in his wire. Right guns (2 section) were particularly effective an enemy bombing party being dispersed with casualties.	CWW
			Front line was attacked briskly with enemy fire of all kinds.	
"	6.7.16		Day was again quiet except for apparent searching for our batteries by enemy artillery & work proceeded without interruption.	CWW
			Fauquissart & Masselot House posts were again shelled heavily at intervals during the night	CWW
			Front line guns again kept gaps in wire well under their fire & at gap 76 dispersed a party that attempted to work there. On the Wick salient a party attempted to repair work but were prevented by our fire.	CWW
			Our right front line guns having been particularly & persistently active lately, enemy artillery violently bombarded their approximate positions at 11.0 pm. but with no success. They were fired at intervals from 9.45 pm to 3.50 am. on the 7th inst. From point M24 d.0.3. indirect searching was applied in direction M24 d 5½ at a searchlight which did not again appear.	CWW CWW

2449 Wt. W14957/M90 750,000 1/16 J.B.C. & A. Forms/C.2118/12.

Instructions regarding War Diaries and Intelligence Summaries are contained in F. S. Regs., Part II. and the Staff Manual respectively. Title Pages will be prepared in manuscript.

WAR DIARY
or
~~INTELLIGENCE SUMMARY~~
(Erase heading not required.)

Army Form C. 2118.

183 M. G. Coy.

Place	Date	Hour	Summary of Events and Information	Remarks and references to Appendices
In the field	7.7.16		Work proceeded quietly through the day.	
		10.0pm	Right front section positions were again subjected to artillery & indirect M. G. fire. Gaps in enemy wire were kept under our fire through the night. Indirect fire was applied to enemy communication from point N14 c 6½, 2½. This was replied to by enemy M. guns who searched for our positions without success. Enemy redoubt at N19 a 8.4 & communication leading up to came under our indirect fire. A machine gun firing from this locality was silenced	CW CW CW
"	8.7.16		Both day & night passed quietly except for enemy shelling in the region of Bay 28, Sally ports 11 & 12, Fauquissart & Masselot House, for a short period. Enemy working party which attempted to operate at gap 36 was dispersed & this specially & other gaps were fired at through the night.	CW
		12 mn.	At 12.0pm. from point M24 d 0.3. our searching fire in the direction M24 d 5½ induced a searchlight to desist from operations & it did not again appear.	CW
"	9.7.16		The day was quiet & work proceeded without interruption.	CW
		4.0pm	Enemy artillery active.	
		6.0pm	" aeroplane passed over Laventie in a westerly direction, shelled by our A. A. guns. No hits were observed.	CW
		10.0pm	Heavy bombardment over whole front by enemy artillery.	CW
		11.30pm	Conflagration observed behind our lines to the right. Fired at by with enemy shrapnel.	CW
			Wire gaps & enemy parapet were again fired at through the night.	CW

2449 Wt. W14957/M90 750,000 1/16 J.B.C. & A. Forms/C.2118/12.

Instructions regarding War Diaries and Intelligence Summaries are contained in F. S. Regs., Part II. and the Staff Manual respectively. Title Pages will be prepared in manuscript.

WAR DIARY
or
~~INTELLIGENCE SUMMARY~~
(Erase heading not required.)

Army Form C. 2118.

183 M. G. Coy.

Place	Date	Hour	Summary of Events and Information	Remarks and references to Appendices
In the field	9.7.16 contd		Enemy patrol dispersed by our fire at N24 d.3.3.	CW
			A working party was observed in rear of N14 a 61. Searching fire was applied successfully.	CW
			Our T.F.Ps were much improved during the day.	CW
"	10.7.16	1230 am.	A mine was sprung by the 2/8th Worcesters in the right sector of the front line. Enemy shelled a battery well in our rear near Laventie from 6.0 am with H.E. Remainder of the day quiet. No 3 section T.F.Ps completed.	CW
		9.45am	T.M.B. taken up position in rear of a M.G. battle emplacement; is removed on report being sent to Brigade Hqrs.	CW
		5.30pm.	Fauquissart Post shelled.	CW
			Much aerial activity during the day. Enemy machine fired at without success.	
			N8d, N14a, N19a, N13d were swept by front line guns during night — special attention being paid to gaps in wire again.	CW
			Working party dispersed at N19 A 2.5.	CW
			Fired on sniper located at N13 d 2.3 who ceased fire.	
			Between 10.15pm & 11.15pm, considerable enemy bombardment of front line.	CW
			Enemy's machine guns have not been so active as usual.	CW
			Enemy trench under construction from N19 c 0 2 to N19 b 3 5, discovered by air reconnaissance, was fired at by the indirect fire of 2 guns during the night.	CW

2449 Wt. W14957/M90 750,000 1/16 J.B.C. & A. Forms/C.2118/12.

WAR DIARY
or
INTELLIGENCE SUMMARY
(Erase heading not required.)

183 M. G. Coy.

Army Form C. 2118.

Instructions regarding War Diaries and Intelligence Summaries are contained in F. S. Regs., Part II. and the Staff Manual respectively. Title Pages will be prepared in manuscript.

Place	Date	Hour	Summary of Events and Information	Remarks and references to Appendices
In the field	11.7.16		Batteries in our zone were fired on by enemy artillery, but our reply was vigorous & the remainder of the day was quiet.	CW
			Great difficulty is experienced in procuring spare lock springs & muzzle cups. The latter appear to be of inferior quality & break so frequently that it has been thought advisable to use the guns without cups against the possible [illegible] need for them later on. We have had no spare lock springs since the guns were issued to us – one breakage on each of 4 guns will put them out of action. These matters have been reported to Bgde. Hqrs. twice & to D.A.D.O.S. frequently, but apparently the complaint is general & the fault is somewhere at home.	CW CW CW
		11.15 pm	During the night the enemy's wire gaps & parapet were targets for our front line guns & at 11.15 pm a searchlight was fired at – it was extinguished & did not reappear.	CW CW
		11.20	At 11.20 pm an enemy m.g. gun opening fire from their front line, was silenced.	CW
			Indirect fire with a swinging traverse was applied by two guns to the road N19 c 3½, 1½ to N19 c Intermittently from 11.0 pm to 2.0 am.	CW
			Two other guns during the same period applied their fire to communication trench which is reported under construction from N20 b 2½ 5 to N14 d ½ 2½. It is thought this was effective as it drew vigorous retaliation, which however was quite non-effective. One gun was firing from one of the emplacements built during the last few days, which was quite hidden.	CW CW
			Indirect fire was also applied to communications in N8d.	
			Our Indirect Fire has been greatly helped by air photographs, the information in which has been invaluable.	CW

2449 Wt. W14957/M90 750,000 1/16 J.B.C. & A. Forms/C.2118/12.

Instructions regarding War Diaries and Intelligence Summaries are contained in F. S. Regs., Part II. and the Staff Manual respectively. Title Pages will be prepared in manuscript.

WAR DIARY
or
~~INTELLIGENCE SUMMARY~~
(Erase heading not required.)

Army Form C. 2118.

183 M. G. Coy.

Place	Date	Hour	Summary of Events and Information	Remarks and references to Appendices
In the field	12.7.16		The day has been very quiet & only routine work has been carried out.	CW
			Supply of lock springs arrived.	CW
			In our right sector at night, front line guns kept enemy gaps in wire & parapet under fire	CW
			One enemy working party on machine gun were effectively fired at.	CW
			Trench at N19 b.0.2 was fired at with indirect fire.	
			Left sector. Our front line guns were very active. Enemy parapet wire were kept under fire, & communications in rear were searched. Patrols reported three times on enemy working parties & one specially on wire; these were swept with fire & many casualties were reported. The flash of an enemy M.G. was observed & fired at with unknown results.	CW.
			Indirect fire was applied N8d area, also to communication trench N20 b 2½ 5½ N14 d ½ ½.	CW
			About 11.0 pm red rockets were sent up from the German line. Nothing apparent happened.	CW
			About 1.0 am heavy action was heard in our distant right.	CW
			A previous impression that M.Gs in the German line were changed has been confirmed by their sudden quietness, & lack of persistence & less accurate knowledge of our positions.	CW
In the field	13.7.16		The impression that relief of enemy M.G.s taken place confirmed as no guns enfiladed Jocks Lodge instead of 3 as previously. Enemy M.G.s on front line much quieter, a little more enemy M.G. activity on Right, searching for our guns doing indirect fire.	CW

2449 Wt. W14957/M90 750,000 1/16 J.B.C. & A. Forms/C.2118/12.

Instructions regarding War Diaries and Intelligence Summaries are contained in F. S. Regs., Part II. and the Staff Manual respectively. Title Pages will be prepared in manuscript.

WAR DIARY
or
~~INTELLIGENCE SUMMARY~~
(Erase heading not required.)

183 M.G Company.

Army Form C. 2118.

Place	Date	Hour	Summary of Events and Information	Remarks and references to Appendices
In the field	13.7.16		All through the night the gaps in the wire were kept under intermittent fire by our M.G's.	
		2am	At 2am an enemy working party was caught by the cross fire of two of our guns judging by the cries the result seemed good. 5000 rounds fired	CW
		11.30 pm	Wiring party dispersed.	CW
		2am	Enemy working party dispersed.	CW
			During the night the enemy's communications in N 8 D were searched by indirect fire, also the new communication trench which air photos disclosed the enemy was working on from N 20 B 2½ 5 to N 14 D ½ ½ also new trench N 19 B 0.2 to N 19 B 3.5. 5 guns were engaged. 7000 Rounds fired	CW
			Enemy M.G Emplacement spotted at N 14 b 5 6.	CW
	14.7.16		Through night gaps & parapet searched	CW
		12.15 am	Enemy working party dispersed.	CW
		"	Our patrol reported enemy patrol out, fired on with good effect.	CW
			Enemy M.G at 14 b 5.6 silenced	CW
			Enemy M.G Emplacement suspected at Sap N 14 A 6½ 5, fired on & silenced, 8000 rounds fired by front line guns	CW
			Indirect fire by 8 guns. Targets. Redoubt N 14 B 4.2. to N 14 B 5.3; N 20 B 2½ 5 to N 14 D ½ ½; N 8 D; N 19 B 0.2 to 19 B 3.5; N 19 A 8.7 to 19 C 7 9 } 15000 Rounds.	CW

Army Form C. 2118.

WAR DIARY
or
~~INTELLIGENCE SUMMARY~~ 183 M. G. Company.

(Erase heading not required.)

Instructions regarding War Diaries and Intelligence Summaries are contained in F. S. Regs., Part II. and the Staff Manual respectively. Title Pages will be prepared in manuscript.

Place	Date	Hour	Summary of Events and Information	Remarks and references to Appendices
In the field	14.7.16	12.30 am to 1.45 am	Road Bend & Mansell Post under heavy artillery fire formed under M G fire as well. This is a new target for the enemy.	CW
	16.7.16		182 M G Co took over Gun positions at ~~[illegible]~~ Mansell House, Sanguinet ~~[illegible]~~ C.R.A., Road Bend & Mansell Post.	CW
			92 M G Co took over gun position in Bay 28.	
			184 do " " " " " Picantin Jocks Lodge, Hants Post & Bay 103	CW
		1.30 pm	This left guns of this Company in Bay 48 Sally Post 11, Ape Dead End.	CW
			Guns in front line fired throughout night	CW
		8.20 pm	Gas put over by troops on our Right, this blew back on to us & we wore Box Respirators for 2½ hours. Heavy enemy shelling as a result.	CW
	18.7.16		Day quiet except for short bombardment of front line left sector at 3 pm. Night quiet.	CW
		11 pm	Enemy M G fired from N14 A 6½ 5 & was silenced by our M G.	CW
		1.30 am	Duel between our M G & enemy M G at N14 b 5.6, after 500 rounds enemy gun silenced.	CW
		2.45 } 4.0 } am	Working parties dispersed opposite Wick Salient.	CW
			Gaps in enemy wire kept under fire throughout night.	

2449 Wt. W14957/M90 750,000 1/16 J.B.C. & A. Forms/C.2118/12.

Army Form C. 2118.

Instructions regarding War Diaries and Intelligence Summaries are contained in F. S. Regs., Part II. and the Staff Manual respectively. Title Pages will be prepared in manuscript.

WAR DIARY
or
~~INTELLIGENCE SUMMARY.~~
(Erase heading not required.)

183 M.G. Co.

Place	Date	Hour	Summary of Events and Information	Remarks and references to Appendices
In the field	17.7.16.		Sections 1 & 3 joined the 2 guns of No 2 Section in the front line ready for proposed attack. The attack was postponed from hour to hour & at night Sects 1 & 3 vacated the line, the day was quiet, Indirect fire positions were strengthened near Dead End to accommodate 6 guns.	CW
		7.0 pm	Enemy bombarded M12D heavily.	CW.
	18.7.16		Secs 1 & 3 in Billets in Laventie. 2 guns in front line, remaining gun teams continued to strengthen I.F. position, day & night quiet, no Indirect fire owing to men being engaged in Indirect fire positions	CW
				CW
	19.7.16.		No. 1 & 3 Sections proceeded to front line ready to go over with Infantry, 2 guns of each to go over with 4th wave of Right & Left Battalion respectively, & remainder to stay in support.	CW
		11am	Artillery Bombardment according to programme.	CW
		6pm	Artillery barrage lifted, infantry unable to get across No Man's Land owing to heavy fire of enemy M.G.'s. &c. Section Officer of No 1 Sec with L/Cpl [illegible] got over parapet with gun to cover flank of our advance but Infantry	CW

2449 Wt. W14957/M90 750,000 1/16 J.B.C. & A. Forms/C.2118/12.

Army Form C. 2118.

WAR DIARY
or
~~INTELLIGENCE SUMMARY~~

(Erase heading not required.)

Instructions regarding War Diaries and Intelligence Summaries are contained in F. S. Regs., Part II. and the Staff Manual respectively. Title Pages will be prepared in manuscript.

183 M.G. Co.

Place	Date	Hour	Summary of Events and Information	Remarks and references to Appendices
In the field	19.7.16	6 pm	owing to heavy fire. He patched up wounded carrying one in, while L/Cpl Worthall remained with gun until nightfall & brought same in. Enemy front line unoccupiable owing to bombardment. During bombardment we suffered 1 officer wounded 3 OR killed 17 OR wounded (1 since died of wounds) Attack fully described in Infantry War Diary.	CW
		9 pm	Sec No 4 Sec relieved No 3 No 2 Sec " No 1.	CW.
	19.7.16	11 pm to 6 pm	Indirect fire with 6 guns on enemy's communication. 35,000 rounds fired at 2.35 message received that enemy retiring over open opposite N 14 1, 4000 rounds fired on this spot. after our barrage lifted the enemy manned his parapet & we were able to pick off some of the enemy with 2 belts fired from our parapet.	CW CW.
	20.7.16		Guns readjusted, 2 in front line 1 Cave 1 ~~[illegible]~~ Dead End 2 in Reserve at Dead End.	CW
		10 pm	Indirect fire applied on enemy's communication at M 12 B 3.4 by 2 guns	CW.

2449 Wt. W14957/M90 750,000 1/16 J.B.C. & A. Forms/C.2118/12.

Instructions regarding War Diaries and Intelligence Summaries are contained in F. S. Regs., Part II. and the Staff Manual respectively. Title Pages will be prepared in manuscript.

WAR DIARY
or
~~INTELLIGENCE SUMMARY~~
(Erase heading not required.)

Army Form C. 2118.

183 M.G. Co.

Place	Date	Hour	Summary of Events and Information	Remarks and references to Appendices
In the field	20/7/16		until 4 am in an endeavour to stop him working on same. 7000 rounds fired	CW.
		2.0 am	Front line guns unable to fire before owing to patrols, at this time fire opened on enemy's parapet & gaps in wire.	
		3.0 pm	Enemy working party unexpectedly appeared & was dispersed with heavy casualties.	CW.
"	21/7/16.		Front line guns fired all night on enemy's parapet & gaps in wire. Indirect fire applied on enemy's supports & communications to prevent him repairing same. 4000 rounds fired. Two NCO's of Company did very commendable work carrying in wounded from No Man's Land in the middle of the afternoon.	CW
		10 pm to 11.20	Enemy MG's active round Dead End.	CW.
"	22/7/16	4.53 pm	Indirect fire applied from M12b 2¼ 4½ on enemy's front line trenches at N14A 6¾ 2½, front line bays were cleared & an MG Officer in front line observed effect of our fire which was successful, enemy replied with H.E. & Shrapnel, unsuccessfully searching for our MG	CW

2449 Wt. W14957/M90 750,000 1/16 J.B.C. & A. Forms/C.2118/12.

Army Form C. 2118.

Instructions regarding War Diaries and Intelligence Summaries are contained in F. S. Regs., Part II. and the Staff Manual respectively. Title Pages will be prepared in manuscript.

WAR DIARY
or
~~INTELLIGENCE~~ SUMMARY
(Erase heading not required.)

183 MG Co.

Place	Date	Hour	Summary of Events and Information	Remarks and references to Appendices
In the field	22.7.16.	12MN to 2AM	Indirect fire applied on enemy's communication trench at 14 B 1.3.	CW
		12MN	Frontline guns could not fire before owing to patrols, fired on gaps in wire & enemy's parapet. Enemy working party dispersed at 14 C 4.9.	CW.
	23.7.16.		Relieving 184 MG Co, guns were placed in Bay 103, Foch's Lodge 2, Hank Post, Piccantin & ~~[illegible]~~.	CW
		12MN	Gun in Sally Port 11 fired on large enemy working party inflicting many casualties.	CW
		1.30 am	A number of the enemy were seen looking over the parapet, an MG traversed the parapet & they got down.	CW
		2.0 am	An enemy MG opened fire from 14 b 5.6, we fired back at it, it was moved from bay to bay, we followed & eventually silenced it.	CW
			Gaps in enemy's wire fired on all night.	CW.
			2 open Emplacements made in front line.	
	24.7.16.		Relieving 182 MG Co, guns were placed in Bay 28 Sausage, Mascot House 2. CRA Road Bend & Mascot Post.	CW.

2449 Wt. W14957/M90 750,000 1/16 J.B.C. & A. Forms/C.2118/12.

Instructions regarding War Diaries and Intelligence Summaries are contained in F. S. Regs., Part II. and the Staff Manual respectively. Title Pages will be prepared in manuscript.

WAR DIARY
or
~~INTELLIGENCE SUMMARY~~
(Erase heading not required.)

Army Form C. 2118.

183 M G Co.

Place	Date	Hour	Summary of Events and Information	Remarks and references to Appendices
In the field	24/7 16.		Guns now at following places. Bay 28 — Hart Pit — Elbe — Dead End 48 — Tanguerard — Fetch Lodge (2) — Picantin. Sally Port 11 — CRA — Road Bend Bay 103 — Marsell Trench (2) — Marsell Pit.	CW.
			Working parties at N13 D 8.5 & N13 D 6.4½ dispersed during night with casualties.	CW
			Gaps in enemy's wire & parapet enfiladed during night	CW
			Large working party on left very persistent, but after [illegible] 3 belts into the middle of them, they ceased to work.	
			Enemy seems to be making strenuous endeavours to mend his wire & a considerable amount of MG fire is being directed on his wiring parties	CW.
			Indirect fire on enemy's Redoubt N19 A 8.4 & communications. ~~[illegible]~~ at enemy's communications N19.C 3.2.	CW.
			at N14 B 8.5½ to N20 A 9.7 & at N20 A 9.7 to N20 B 1¾ 5¾ — 4 guns in all.	CW.
	25/7 16.		The four guns at Picantin, Dead End, Marsell Post & Road Bend were withdrawn into rest. Limbers being packed ready for immediate action & the section being billeted & warned to be in a state of readiness	CW.

2449 Wt. W14957/M90 750,000 1/16 J.B.C. & A. Forms/C.2118/12.

Instructions regarding War Diaries and Intelligence Summaries are contained in F. S. Regs., Part II. and the Staff Manual respectively. Title Pages will be prepared in manuscript.

WAR DIARY
or
~~INTELLIGENCE SUMMARY~~

(Erase heading not required.)

Army Form C. 2118.

183 M G Co.

Place	Date	Hour	Summary of Events and Information	Remarks and references to Appendices
In the field	25.7.16.		to man the posts if called upon.	CW.
			Front line guns fired on gaps in enemy's wire & searched his parapet. Covered our patrols	CW
			Front line guns fired on & caused casualties amongst 5 enemy working parties during night, at N13D 6.4½ N13D 8.5 N13D 2.5. N13D 7.5 N13D 9.6½	CW.
		12.30 am	Large wiring party endeavouring to mend gap F3 dispersed with casualties.	CW
		1.0 am	Belt fired on enemy searchlight which ceased to shine	CW.
			Indirect fire applied on roads N15A 2.6 to N14B 6.1 N20A 9.7 to N20B 1¾ 5¾	CW
			Front line trenches greatly strengthened & repaired by R.E. & Infantry	CW
	26.7.16		Front line guns fired on gaps in enemy's wire & on parapet.	CW.
			Indirect fire. Artillery reported that large bodies of enemy crossed the Stream at N15C 1.9. 2 guns placed on this point with short bursts all night. Enemy very quiet	CW.

2449 Wt. W14957/M90 750,000 1/16 J.B.C. & A. Forms/C.2118/12.

Instructions regarding War Diaries and Intelligence Summaries are contained in F. S. Regs., Part II. and the Staff Manual respectively. Title Pages will be prepared in manuscript.

WAR DIARY
or
INTELLIGENCE SUMMARY
(Erase heading not required.)

Army Form C. 2118.

183 M G Co.

Place	Date	Hour	Summary of Events and Information	Remarks and references to Appendices
In the field	27.4.16	6.0 am. to 8.30 am	Indirect fire in conjunction with Artillery TM's brought to bear on Wick Salient, 2500 rounds fired.	CW
			One front line guns enfiladed Salient from behind our parados & fired 1500 rounds.	CW.
		5 pm	Indirect fire applied on point which Artillery informed us of N 15 c 1.9 until 10 pm. Ration parties were seen crossing about this time on previous nights.	CW
		9 pm to 10 am	During night I F applied on enemy's new trench N 19 B 0.2 to 19 B 2½ 6. 3500 rounds enemy replied with M. G. fire.	CW
		11 pm	Heavy bombardment on right.	CW
			Front line guns active all night playing on enemy's parapet & gaps.	CW.
			A considerable amount of work was done on new emplacements for Indirect fire	CW
	28.4.16.		Owing to Patrol & wiring party being out opposite Bay 48 1 gun was unable to fire. Others guns kept were open, & fired at gaps. Indirect Fire by Masselot Post enfiladed Wick Salient from both flanks.	CW

2449 Wt. W14957/M90 750,000 1/16 J.B.C. & A. Forms/C.2118/12.

Instructions regarding War Diaries and Intelligence Summaries are contained in F. S. Regs., Part II. and the Staff Manual respectively. Title Pages will be prepared in manuscript.

WAR DIARY

or

~~INTELLIGENCE SUMMARY~~

(Erase heading not required.)

Army Form C. 2118.

183 M.G. Coy

Place	Date	Hour	Summary of Events and Information	Remarks and references to Appendices
In the Field	29/7/16		No firing during day; our front line guns firing intermittently at gaps in Enemy's wire & swept his parapet. Owing to mist results not observed. Front line guns lifted on enemy communication running up from N22 a 1c 6c	CW
		10.25 to 11.15 pm	4 Guns cooperating with Artillery & T.M.B's applied indirect fire along lines N14 b 1 2 to N8 d 9 1 & N8 d 5. 2½ to N19 C 10. 0 & in rear of these. During night material for new emplacements conveyed to Rue Tilleloy. ~~at~~	CW
	30/7/16		Owing to presence of our own working parties our front line guns could not fire until 2.0 when ~~both~~ 2 guns traversed enemy's parapet & fired on gaps in wire 2200 rds. Wick Salient was enfiladed in conjunction with Lewis guns.	CW
		3.0 am	Enemy working party dispersed	CW
			Indirect Fire with two guns searching Rue Delvaal 2,500 rds.	CW
	31/7/16		Day was quiet except for sharp artillery duel battery near Masselot House taking part.	CW
			At night Front line guns were actively engaged on enemy's parapet & gaps in his wire.	CW
		11.0 to 11.30 pm	Large parties of enemy reported in No Mans Land, fire directed on these & thought to be effective, it not being possible to observe clearly owing to mist.	CW

2449 Wt. W14957/M90 750,000 1/16 J.B.C. & A. Forms/C.2118/12.

Army Form C. 2118.

Instructions regarding War Diaries and Intelligence Summaries are contained in F. S. Regs., Part II. and the Staff Manual respectively. Title Pages will be prepared in manuscript.

WAR DIARY
or
~~INTELLIGENCE SUMMARY~~
(Erase heading not required.)

183 M. G. Coy.

Place	Date	Hour	Summary of Events and Information	Remarks and references to Appendices
In the Field	31/7/16		Indirect fire applied from the right to "Rue d'Enfer" communication, Distillery, & tracks across 19B.	CW

C. M. Walker Capt.
Commdg 183 M.G. Co.

2449 Wt. W14957/M90 750,000 1/16 J.B.C. & A. Forms/C.2118/12.

Vol 3

183rd Inf. BDE

War Diary

- of -

183 Machine Gun Coy

Augt 1st - 31st 1916

Instructions regarding War Diaries and Intelligence Summaries are contained in F. S. Regs., Part II. and the Staff Manual respectively. Title Pages will be prepared in manuscript.

WAR DIARY
or
~~INTELLIGENCE SUMMARY~~
(Erase heading not required.)

183 M. G. Coy

Army Form C. 2.

Place	Date	Hour	Summary of Events and Information	Remarks and references to Appendices
In the Field	Aug 1 1916	6.0 am	Fired on enemy working party with extreme left hand gun with excellent effect making them cease work.	CW
			Day was quiet except for artillery duels	
		11.30 pm	Last night kept enemy line under intermittant fire & from Bay 103 we fired on & dispersed a working party & patrol	CW
			~~The~~ Enemy fire from Machine Guns was directed along our front line the fire it is thought was indirect at a considerable range	CW
			The source of fire could not be observed	CW
			Indirect fire was applied by our guns near Masselot House to road from 20A 9.7 to 20 D10.3 although enemy MGuns replied & our gun was hit fire was persisted in. This strong retaliation on the part of the enemy points to our fire being effective	CW
		11 pm to 2.0 am		CW
	Aug 2 1916		The day was fairly quiet.	
		12.30 am	Enemy shelled vicinity of Masselot House which received direct hit. Indirect fire was brought to bear on enemy communication in N14 b & especially N14 6 7.6	CW
			Front line guns fired on enemy line during night, & fire effectively on working parties at N8D3½ 1½ & N14B2½ 9½.	CW

2449 Wt. W14957/M90 750,000 1/16 J.B.C. & A. Forms/C.2118/12.

Army Form C. 2118.

Instructions regarding War Diaries and Intelligence Summaries are contained in F. S. Regs., Part II. and the Staff Manual respectively. Title Pages will be prepared in manuscript.

WAR DIARY
or
~~INTELLIGENCE SUMMARY~~
(Erase heading not required.)

183 M. G. Coy

Place	Date	Hour	Summary of Events and Information	Remarks and references to Appendices
In the Field	Aug 3rd 1916		Front line guns fired during night on enemy's wire, gaps & parapet 3,500 rds	CW
			Enemy concrete M.G. Emplacement discovered at N19a 3.1. This was passed on to Artillery who shelled it while our guns fired on it.	CW
		2.15 am	Enemy M.G. firing from parapet silenced	CW
			A M.G. emplacement located near Wick Sal: our guns silenced this gun as soon as he fired	CW
			Enemy Working parties round Wick Salient very active & persistent One was dispersed with casualties. All night fire was kept on the front of the Salient to stop these parties. It was suggested that one or two Lewis guns might fire on the Salient as the enemy was making desperate efforts to repair his wire there.	CW
			Indirect Fire	
			2 Guns on communications leading to N19 b 3.2 & the road in short bursts 2500 rds	CW
			2 guns on the communications leading up to Wick Salient firing in short bursts 2,500 rds	CW
			Work Done	
			Emplacement in [illegible] Area: resighted. Assisting R.E's to build M.G. dugouts in front line also 2 new Emplacements.	CW

2449 Wt. W14957/M90 750,000 1/16 J.B.C. & A. Forms/C.2118/12.

Army Form C. 2118.

WAR DIARY
or
~~INTELLIGENCE SUMMARY~~

(Erase heading not required.)

Instructions regarding War Diaries and Intelligence Summaries are contained in F. S. Regs., Part II. and the Staff Manual respectively. Title Pages will be prepared in manuscript.

183. M. G. Coy

Place	Date	Hour	Summary of Events and Information	Remarks and references to Appendices
In the Field	4/8/16		Front Line guns on the right fired 4,000 rds on gaps traversing enemy parapet & enfilading Sugar Loaf. On the left our guns silenced open emplacement at N 13 d 7.5 also fired on gaps in wire & traversed enemy parapet. Enemy MG Emplacement N19 c 2.8 fired on & gun silenced. Enemy's supports searched by these guns. During early hours of the morning IF was applied at the new trench N19 B 0.2 to N19 B 3 5½. The day & night were very quiet except in the morning 4.8.16 when the enemy shelled around Sally Port 12 heavily ~~[illegible]~~ almost getting a direct hit on the emplacement the infantry wisely withdrew leaving the defence in the hands of the team of 1 Vickers gun. I note that the Lewis Guns report stoppages & whether they are cleared or not. One clears too many on Vickers guns in one night for me to give you these in detail.	
	5/8/16		Front line guns fired through night at enemy's parapet & gaps in wire. 7,500 rds in all.	
		10.30 pm – 2.0 am	Enemy working parties at Week dispersed.	
			M. G. at N19 c 2.8 again fired but was eventually silenced	
			Enemy working parties at F.26 dispersed with casualties	
		12.15.	Infantry reported that an enemy ~~working~~ raiding party was coming from F11 direction we emptied 4 belts in that direction into No Mans Land, and as no more was heard of alleged raid	

Army Form C. 2118.

WAR DIARY
or
~~INTELLIGENCE SUMMARY~~
(Erase heading not required.)

Instructions regarding War Diaries and Intelligence Summaries are contained in F. S. Regs., Part II. and the Staff Manual respectively. Title Pages will be prepared in manuscript.

183 M. G. Coy

Place	Date	Hour	Summary of Events and Information	Remarks and references to Appendices
In the Field	5/8/16		trust we limed the invader	
			Indirect fire on enemys trench N19B 0.3 to N19B 3.6 2000 yds	
			CRA heavily shelled during day. Machine guns very active on both sides last night.	
		6pm	Our aeroplanes proceeding over our lines were fired on one machine was hit & came to the ground	
		9pm	Big fire noticed in direction of Neuve Chapelle, this was burning until 12.15 pm	
			New emplacement at Bay 28 sighted	
			More work done on new M.G. Emplacements & dugouts	
	6/8/16		Front Line guns fired on gaps in enemys wire & on parapet	
		10.30 pm & 1.30	Working parties near gap F6 were fired on with believed casualties; also another working party near Wick was dispersed. Two parties were caught one near F2A & the other on the Sugar Loaf. It is thought some of these were hit.	
			Owing to internal reliefs no indirect fire was done last night. New dugouts for M.Gs in front line were proceeded with also all new Emplacements; position for new Emplacement in Bay 64 arranged in conjunction with R.E.s	
			Night very quiet	

2449 Wt. W14957/M90 750,000 1/16 J.B.C. & A. Forms/C.2118/12.

Instructions regarding War Diaries and Intelligence Summaries are contained in F. S. Regs., Part II. and the Staff Manual respectively. Title Pages will be prepared in manuscript.

WAR DIARY
or
~~INTELLIGENCE SUMMARY~~
(Erase heading not required.)

183 M.G. Co

Army Form C. 2118.

Place	Date	Hour	Summary of Events and Information	Remarks and references to Appendices
In the Field	7/8/16	10pm to 1am	Front Line guns firing on parapet provided flanking fire for Raiding Party, & later fired as usual on gaps & parapet. 2 Enemy working parties dispersed on Wick 3,000 rds, also working parties ½ Right from Bay 48	
			Indirect fire for Raiding Party Barrage about N19 3½ 1½ & Indirect fire at N13d 1½ 1 & N19 c. 3.2	
		10.30 pm to 12.45 am	5250 rds were fired	[initials]
		6.45 am	Masselot House was Bombarded by hostile aeroplanes	
	8/8/16		Front line guns dispersed 3 working parties around Wick Salient & an enemy patrol opposite Bay 10 was fired on.	
		1.0 am	We followed an enemy M.G. from Bay to Bay & eventually he ceased to fire.	
			Wiring party dispersed near Sugar Loaf	
		4.30 am	Large working party was seen opposite Rhondda Sap. This was traversed & men seen to fall.	[initials]
			Gaps in wire fired on & parapets traversed	
			2 guns did Indirect fire on the Rue Delaval	
			Work on new emplacements & dugouts continued	

2449 Wt. W14957/M90 750,000 1/16 J.B.C. & A. Forms/C.2118/12.

Instructions regarding War Diaries and Intelligence Summaries are contained in F. S. Regs., Part II. and the Staff Manual respectively. Title Pages will be prepared in manuscript.

WAR DIARY
or
~~INTELLIGENCE SUMMARY~~
(Erase heading not required.)

Army Form C. 2118.

183 M. G. Co

Place	Date	Hour	Summary of Events and Information	Remarks and references to Appendices
In the Field	9/8/16		This company was relieved by 184 M.G. C. We supplied guides for the relieving gunteams to their respective positions. The men were then marched back to billets. Men marched to billets at Lestrem previously occupied by 184 M.G. Co	[initials]
	10/8/16		Materiel was packed, & the quarters were thoroughly cleaned & tidied up before leaving. ~~The company then marched to the quarters previously occupied by 184 M.G.C. at Lestrem the sections being appointed to various parts of billets.~~ Stores etc unpacked & stored. General cleaning up, guns & rifles etc	[initials]
	11/8/16	am 6.30 to 10.30	Bathing Parade constituting route march there & back.	[initials]
		1.0	Elementary Drill 1 Section attached to Worcesters for Combined ~~[illegible]~~ attack practise.	
		2.0	Stoppages. *	
	12/8/16	6-6.30 am	Physical Drill } 2 Section 2 Section on Constructing Range	[initials]
		8-9	Mechanism }	
		9-10	Infantry Drill }	
	13/8/16	10-11.30	Fixing up Pack Mules	
		3 pm	1 Officer & 5 O.R's proceeded to Camiers for advanced M.G. Course	[initials]
	14/8/16	6-6.30	Physical Drill } by 2 Sections 2 sections on Constructing M.G. Range	
		8-9.0	Infantry Drill }	
		9.0-11.30	Advanced Drill } Transport under Transport Officer for instruction	

Instructions regarding War Diaries and Intelligence Summaries are contained in F. S. Regs., Part II. and the Staff Manual respectively. Title Pages will be prepared in manuscript.

WAR DIARY
or
~~INTELLIGENCE SUMMARY~~ 183 M.G. Co

(Erase heading not required.)

Army Form C. 2118.

Place	Date	Hour	Summary of Events and Information	Remarks and references to Appendices
In the Field	15/8/16		Constructing Range	
			Recruits attend Gas Lecture & demonstration	
			1 Officer & 4 N.C.O's at Gas School.	[illegible]
			2nd Lt. E. E. Smith reported for duty from M.G.C. Base Depot	
	16/8/16	6–6.30	Physical Drill. Inspection of Harness.	
		8–10	Action from Limbers	
		10–10.30	Lecture on Indirect Fire with demonstration	[illegible]
		11.30 to 11.30	Stoppages. 1 Section attached Infantry battalion for combined attack practise.	
	17/8/16	6–6.30	Physical Drill	
		8–9	Manual	
		9 to 11.30	Advanced Drill. Transport Waggon Drill & Tactical Lecture.	[illegible]
	18/8/16		Stores & materiel etc packed, & company marched to R 35 c 10.8. Unpacked & prepared place for occupation. We relieved 94 M.G. C on Richebourg front.	[illegible]
	19/8/16		Front line gun fired 1750 rds on enemy's parapet & gaps in wire except between 12 MN & 1.30 AM when ~~they~~ it ceased owing to ~~presence~~ presence of patrols.	[illegible]

2449 Wt. W14957/M90 750,000 1/16 J.B.C. & A. Forms/C.2118/12.

Army Form C. 2118.

WAR DIARY
or
~~INTELLIGENCE SUMMARY~~

(Erase heading not required.)

Instructions regarding War Diaries and Intelligence Summaries are contained in F. S. Regs., Part II. and the Staff Manual respectively. Title Pages will be prepared in manuscript.

183 MG Co.

Place	Date	Hour	Summary of Events and Information	Remarks and references to Appendices
In the Field	19/8/16		Indirect Fire from Pont Logy on La Russe 56 d 5.9 with two guns 3,000 rds	[initials]
			Night very quiet but heavy bombardment on left	
			Great many MG's fired at our aircraft.	
	20/8/16		Front line gun fired 2,000 rds on enemys parapet & gaps	
			Enemy's MG's active on posts & roads, & artillery a little more active.	
		8.30 am	A number of Rifle Grenades sent over at Copse Post	
			Indirect Fire. A shoot in combination with 182 MG Co in which our TMB's joined commenced at 10pm & finished at 11.30pm 6 guns in IF position near Pont Logy fired on Southern half of Bois de Biez. The guns were to have fired until 1am but at 11.30pm owing to heavy MG fire the place got too hot & we had to withdraw	[initials]
		11pm	Two whiz bangs fell within 10yds of two guns.	
		8.15pm	Enemy aeroplane dropped 3 bombs near Pont Logy two exploded but did no damage, the aeroplane then returned.	

2449 Wt. W14957/M90 750,000 1/16 J.B.C. & A. Forms/C.2118/12.

Instructions regarding War Diaries and Intelligence Summaries are contained in F. S. Regs., Part II. and the Staff Manual respectively. Title Pages will be prepared in manuscript.

WAR DIARY
or
~~INTELLIGENCE SUMMARY~~
(Erase heading not required.)

Army Form C. 2118.

183 M G Coy.

Place	Date	Hour	Summary of Events and Information	Remarks and references to Appendices
In the Field	21/8/16	11 pm	Enemy working party dispersed with known Casualties at S10 d 7.8. 2000 rds were fired on enemy's parapet & gaps.	
		pm 11.15 to 11.30	Our gun position bombarded with T M's on both sides.	
		1 am	Searchlight seen. Fired on it with result that it ceased shining. The enemy put up several red lights, during the night. Enemy's M G's very active. No indirect fire was done as positions were untenable. Fresh places are being reconnoitred & indirect will be done tonight.	[initials]
	22/8/16		Fired about 2,000 rds on enemy's parapet & wire. It was much too misty to observe working parties.	
		pm 9.15	A number of HE's fell in close proximity to Lansdowne Post. Indirect Fire with 2 guns was directed ~~on S3A 7.5½~~ on enemy's front line from S3A 7.5½. Fired 3,000 rds. Enemy did not retaliate.	[initials]
	23/8/16	9.30 pm	Considerable artillery activity on our side occasioned heavy retaliation on our front line & rear posts.	
		am 12.30	Bombardment renewed which drew still further heavy retaliation	[initials]

2449 Wt. W14957/M90 750,000 1/16 J.B.C. & A. Forms/C.2118/12.

Army Form C. 2118.

Instructions regarding War Diaries and Intelligence Summaries are contained in F. S. Regs., Part II. and the Staff Manual respectively. Title Pages will be prepared in manuscript.

WAR DIARY
or
~~INTELLIGENCE~~ SUMMARY
(Erase heading not required.)

183 M G Co

Place	Date	Hour	Summary of Events and Information	Remarks and references to Appendices
In the Field	23/8/16		Pont Logy received some attention from H Es & Shrapnel Bay 63 sustained considerable damage but repairing operations are being pushed forward at once. Front line guns fired on enemys front line & wire During night Indirect Fire was applied from vicinity of Pont Logy on enemy communications in region of the La Bassee Rd. Enemy M Gs were active.	[illegible]
	24/8/16	11pm/1am	Front line guns fired on enemys parapet & gaps especially at re entrant at S11A & C. 1750 rds fired. No firing took place owing to presence of our patrols. ~~17~~ No Indirect Fire owing to orders of B G C B Work done Indirect Fire positions strengthened	[illegible]
	25/8/16		Front line guns fired on enemys front line & wire 2250 rds No targets presented themselves & so a steady M G fire was maintained on enemy parapet. No indirect fire was done; there are no Indirect Fire positions at all & considerable work will be needed to make any good if possible.	[illegible]

2449 Wt. W14957/M90 750,000 1/16 J.B.C. & A. Forms/C.2118/12.

Instructions regarding War Diaries and Intelligence Summaries are contained in F. S. Regs., Part II. and the Staff Manual respectively. Title Pages will be prepared in manuscript.

Army Form C. 2118.

WAR DIARY
or
~~INTELLIGENCE SUMMARY~~
(Erase heading not required.)

183 MGCo

Place	Date	Hour	Summary of Events and Information	Remarks and references to Appendices
In the Field	26/8/16	7.30 pm	In reply to our TM activity the enemy shelled heavily bay by No 9 gun at Emplacement #22 (x) One man is reported killed who went to a near bay to assist wounded.	
			During the night an enemy MG fired from M30A55 The flash was observed & one of the guns carefully laid; on his reopening fire we also fired & the appears to have concluded his work for the night	
			Front line guns fired on enemy parapet & gaps	
	27/8/16		Day was quiet except for enemy retaliation to our TMB activity in the late afternoon. Our guns did indirect fire on Bois du Biez at this time	
		10 pm 12 MN	3000 rds were fired traversing from M30B 0 5½ to M30C 0.6	
			Front line guns fired on enemy parapet & wire.	
		12 MN	Working party dispersed at M36A 2.5.	
			Enemy communications at M30A C & d were searched at intervals	
			Moated Grange was the object of considerable enemy MG fire during afternoon.	
			An open emplacement has been prepared during day in Front Line	

2449 Wt. W14957/M90 750,000 1/16 J.B.C. & A. Forms/C.2118/12.

Army Form C. 2118.

Instructions regarding War Diaries and Intelligence Summaries are contained in F. S. Regs., Part II. and the Staff Manual respectively. Title Pages will be prepared in manuscript.

WAR DIARY
or
~~INTELLIGENCE SUMMARY~~
(Erase heading not required.)

183 M.G. Co

Place	Date	Hour	Summary of Events and Information	Remarks and references to Appendices
In the Field	28/9/16	10pm	Front line guns maintained steady fire on enemy's parapet & wire. In front of Bay 232 a working party was fired on with believed casualties (3,500 rds.) An enemy MG was chased & eventually quietened at M36 A 3.2. Fired on communication Trench at M30 d 5.1½ Bursts on enemys wire & parapet. 3 guns. 3500 rds. one gun could not fire after 10.30pm because of our patrols. Indirect fire at 4.0pm in conjunction with Artillery programme, 2 guns fired on enemys trenches in M30 d. At 4.45 2 more guns fired enfilading trenches M30 A 8.3 to M24 d 9.5 & trenches in M30 c	[illegible]
		4.51 4.56	All guns fired on trenches in M30 D. 6000 rds fired in all. Two of these guns had to move their positions as several shells fell within 50 yds & one about 10 yds away. They were firing from an indirect fire position near Winchester, & moved & resumed firing. Moated Grange & Chateau Redoubt had direct hits yesterday.	

2449 Wt. W14957/M90 750,000 1/16 J.B.C. & A. Forms/C.2118/12.

Instructions regarding War Diaries and Intelligence Summaries are contained in F. S. Regs., Part II. and the Staff Manual respectively. Title Pages will be prepared in manuscript.

WAR DIARY
or
~~INTELLIGENCE~~ SUMMARY

(Erase heading not required.)

183 M G Co

Army Form C. 2118.

Place	Date	Hour	Summary of Events and Information	Remarks and references to Appendices
~~[illegible]~~ In the Field	29/8/16		Front Line guns fired 4,000 rds on enemys parapet + wire gaps. One working party opposite Bay 232 was moved. One gun on left could not fire owing to our patrol being out. Working party opposite M.G. Emplac received a belt from us, which resulted in the enemy blowing his stretcher bearer horns rather vigourously.	
			Considerable + heavy Artillery activity during the night + during the day Chateau Keep received more directs + moated Grange was also shelled.	[initials]
			During the afternoon alot of light shells fell near Winchester Post.	
			The heavy rains made some of the dugouts + emplacements exceedingly uncomfortable.	
	31/8/16		Front line guns searched enemys parapet + gaps in wire + at intervals lifting to communication.	
			Enemy M.G. opposite 32 was fired on with good effect as it was not observed to fire again during the evening	[initials]
		10pm to 2am	One gun on right unable to fire owing to presence of our patrols No of rds fired 3,000.	

2449 Wt. W14957/M90 750,000 1/16 J.B.C. & A. Forms/C.2118/12.

Instructions regarding War Diaries and Intelligence Summaries are contained in F. S. Regs., Part II. and the Staff Manual respectively. Title Pages will be prepared in manuscript.

WAR DIARY
or
~~INTELLIGENCE SUMMARY~~

(Erase heading not required.)

Army Form C. 2118.

183 M G Co

Place	Date	Hour	Summary of Events and Information	Remarks and references to Appendices
In the Field.	31/8/16		Moated Grange was shelled twice during the afternoon. Indirect Fire was carried out on the following points. M30 D 9.7 M31A 3.3 Enfilading enemy trench M30 B 0.5 to M24 D. 10.6. + left of half of Bois du Biez. Guns fired from 1.38 am to 2.10 am + fired in all 5,000 rds	[initials]
	30/8/16		The day was quiet till the late afternoon when there was artillery + TM activity from our side. Enemy artillery dropped 6 heavy shells on Hush Hall demolishing half of it + spoiling a dugout but failing to penetrate the steel lining	
		9.9 pm to 12 mn	Fire was applied to M36 d 5½ 6 + surrounding buildings + occasionally traversing round from Pietro S.W.	[initials]
			Front Line guns fired as usual	
		am 12.00	Gun at 21 Emplace got a good target due south, dispersing an enemy working party precipitately with casualties. Enemy M.G. fired on as per I.P. Report August 26-27 has not been observed to fire from his position since.	

C.M.Walker Capt
OC 183 M.G.Co.

2449 Wt. W14957/M90 750,000 1/16 J.B.C. & A. Forms/C.2118/12.

183rd Infantry Brigade

Vol 4

War Diary

of

183rd Machine Gun Company

for

September 1916.

Instructions regarding War Diaries and Intelligence Summaries are contained in F. S. Regs., Part II. and the Staff Manual respectively. Title Pages will be prepared in manuscript.

WAR DIARY
or
~~INTELLIGENCE SUMMARY~~
(Erase heading not required.)

183 M.G. Coy

Army Form C. 2118.

Place	Date	Hour	Summary of Events and Information	Remarks and references to Appendices
In the Field	Sept 1st 1916	12 noon	Moated Grange was fairly heavily shelled for ½ hour when the side wall was hit & after a short cessation shelling recommenced & a heavy shell (estimated 5.9) landed on the roof and the emplacement requires engineer assistance to repair. Shelling continued for 2 hours. Heavy shells were also dropped about 200 yds left of Hush Hall; target was not obvious and no serious damage was done.	
			Front line guns fired as usual. On left gun from Post 21 after duel with enemy MG at M36d 2 7 silenced it at about 11.0 pm.	
		1.45 am	Working party at M36a 3.4 was dispersed with observed casualties.	
		9.15 pm	Gun from Post 22 dispersed an enemy working party at M36a 4.0 and stretcher bearers horn was sounded. It is believed casualties were inflicted. A working party was again observed at this point & dispersed with accurate fire.	
		am 1.0 to 2.0	An enemy MG at about M36c. 2.8 was fired on and silenced.	

2449 Wt. W14957/M90 750,000 1/16 J.B.C. & A. Forms/C.2118/12.

Army Form C. 2118.

Instructions regarding War Diaries and Intelligence Summaries are contained in F. S. Regs., Part II. and the Staff Manual respectively. Title Pages will be prepared in manuscript.

WAR DIARY
or
~~INTELLIGENCE SUMMARY~~
(Erase heading not required.)

183 M.G. Co.

Place	Date	Hour	Summary of Events and Information	Remarks and references to Appendices
In the Field.	2/9/16		Front line guns fired as usual on enemys gaps in wire & on parapets	
			On right gun fired on OP situated at S5b 6¼ 2¾ reported in Corps Summary of Information.	
			The enemy in the sector opposite Bay 170 fired no shots & put up no Very Lights.	
		12 am	Order 'Gas Alert' was received	
		10 pm	Working party dispersed at M30c 5.6.	
		2.30 am	Same party reappeared & was dispersed.	
			The enemy seems to have a great desire to do work at this point.	
			A flash was seen to come from M36 a.4.6 it was thought to come from a Trench Mortar Battery & 250 r[illegible] were fired on it as quickly as possible; the flash did not reappear.	[illegible]
			Indirect Fire. Rue d'Enfer was systematically searched last night with 2 guns for 4 hours. 2,500 rds were fired	
			Moated Grange was heavily shelled during morning & afternoon.	

2449 Wt. W14957/M90 750,000 1/16 J.B.C. & A. Forms/C.2118/12.

Army Form C. 2118.

WAR DIARY
or
~~INTELLIGENCE SUMMARY~~

(Erase heading not required.)

183 M.G. Co.

Instructions regarding War Diaries and Intelligence Summaries are contained in F. S. Regs., Part II. and the Staff Manual respectively. Title Pages will be prepared in manuscript.

Place	Date	Hour	Summary of Events and Information	Remarks and references to Appendices
In the Field	2/9/16		Work done Considerable work has been done rendering billets suitable for winter quarters.	
	3/9/16		Positions No 9 & 10 & Chateau were relieved by 94 M.G. Coy in the morning Brickfields after dark & Position 11 in the front line on the left & Cinema House were taken over by us from 184 M.G. Co.	
		12 noon 2pm 4pm	Artillery & TM's fired on the enemy drawing retaliation which so far as can be observed did little damage. Indirect Fire was applied at 2.2, 4.2 & 6.2 pm on enemy front line & reserve lines in M30b & M24d. There was no retaliation on our gun positions.	
	4/9/16	10am to 10.30	Front line guns fired as usual – about 4,000 rds. Indirect Fire was applied to communications in M30d & also M36 b1.7 to M36 b 0.2½. About 3 MTM's were put over from this side in cooperation. The enemy replied with a few TM's on our front line. Front line guns fired as usual through the night expending about 4,000 rounds	

2449 Wt. W14957/M90 750,000 1/16 J.B.C. & A. Forms/C.2118/12.

Instructions regarding War Diaries and Intelligence Summaries are contained in F. S. Regs., Part II. and the Staff Manual respectively. Title Pages will be prepared in manuscript.

WAR DIARY
or
~~INTELLIGENCE SUMMARY~~
(Erase heading not required.)

183 M.G. Co

Army Form C. 2118.

Place	Date	Hour	Summary of Events and Information	Remarks and references to Appendices
In the Field	4/9/16	12 mn	A working party was found & dispersed at M30c 5.5.	
			The night & day was exceptionally quiet	
	5/9/16	pm 4.0	Indirect Fire was applied on a line M30.69.0 – M30d.0.6	
		4.30		
		9.0pm	Further Indirect fire against cross roads M31a 1.3 was applied in short bursts till about 11 pm. Enemy M.G: searched in reply.	
			The work of front line guns was somewhat limited by the work of our patrols, but swept the enemy parapet & wire during the available intervals till day break	
			About 4,000 rds were fired.	
			The whole day & night were comparatively quiet.	
	6/9/16	pm 9.30	Indirect Fire was applied to communication at M30c9.7 with occasional bursts of swinging traverse in M30d	
		pm 10.45	Indirect Fire was stopped on receipt of operation orders	
		pm 10.45 12.15	The artillery was very active at this period, & drew only slight retaliation	
		pm 11.0	Enemy M.G.s were fairly active	
			One of our sentries reported a bright light towards Laventie in the sky, which fell & grew more intense as it approached the ground	

2449 Wt. W14957/M90 750,000 1/16 J.B.C. & A. Forms/C.2118/12.

2449 Wt. W14957/M90 750,000 1/16 J.B.C. & A. Forms/C.2118/12.

Army Form C. 2118.

WAR DIARY
or
~~INTELLIGENCE SUMMARY~~
(Erase heading not required.)

183 M.G. Co.

Instructions regarding War Diaries and Intelligence Summaries are contained in F. S. Regs., Part II. and the Staff Manual respectively. Title Pages will be prepared in manuscript.

Place	Date	Hour	Summary of Events and Information	Remarks and references to Appendices
In the Field	6/9/16		Front line guns swept enemy wire & parapet with fire before & after our ~~parapet~~ patrols went out.	
		pm 10.20	Infantry reported an enemy bombing party. This was fired on at M24 d5.1 & disappeared.	
			Work has been done to improve Moated Grange but the M.G. E. which suffered a direct hit is badly in need of repair. This can hardly be done by us without R.E. supervision.	[illegible]
	7/9/16	pm 9.15 9.35 & 9.40 9.50	Indirect Fire was applied to M30 c 9.7. (dugout work) and also to the left flank of Bois du Biez – group of trenches around S6.7.2	
		am 9.0 12.0 2.0 4.45	Indirect Fire was also applied to search enemy communications M25 c 7.1 to M30 d. 8.7. to traverse M.25.7.1. – M31 a 0.2 M31 a 0.2 – S6 a 5.3	
			Enemy M Gs swept Rue Tilleloy in rear of some of our guns about 9.0 & 9.30 pm. This did not interfere with the programme.	[illegible]
			Front line guns fired as usual. Very little was heard of enemy fire on the front all night	

2449 Wt. W14957/M90 750,000 1/16 J.B.C. & A. Forms/C.2118/12.

Instructions regarding War Diaries and Intelligence Summaries are contained in F. S. Regs., Part II. and the Staff Manual respectively. Title Pages will be prepared in manuscript.

WAR DIARY
or
~~INTELLIGENCE SUMMARY~~

(Erase heading not required.)

Army Form C. 2118.

183 M G Co.

Place	Date	Hour	Summary of Events and Information	Remarks and references to Appendices
In the Field.	8/9/16		The day was fairly quiet but Moated Grange was shelled	
		am 5.0 to 6.0	during the morning from 10.30 – 11.30 am. It was again shelled, & no direct hits were registered	
		8-9	on the emplacement	
		pm 8.45	Our artillery were very active & red rockets were seen to go up from enemy line.	
		pm 8.45 to 9.45	Indirect Fire was applied as follows	
			1 M 25 a 1 ½ – M 30 d 8.7 – M 30 b 8 2 – M 30 d 5.6 Area	
			2 M 19 c 3 ½ – M 25 b 5.1 Line.	
			3. M 25 a 6.6 Les Mottes Fermes.	
			4. M 30 d 9.7 – M 25 c 7.1 Line	
			5 S 6 a 9.9 – S 6 a 4.2 – S 6 b 2.8 – S 6 a 7.0	
		pm 10.15 to 11.45	Targets 1 & 2 were again fired on.	[initials]
		pm 9.30	A report was received that our I.F. was hitting our front line in the sector occupied by our right company This was at once investigated & it is thought that this fire must have come from a flank company as our shots passed over Neuve Chappelle occupied by the left over our Flank Brigade. Our guns were not firing at the time	
		pm 9.0 to 9.30	Our positions at Winchester were fired on by enemy M.Gs but without success	

2449 Wt. W14957/M90 750,000 1/16 J.B.C. & A. Forms/C.2118/12.

Instructions regarding War Diaries and Intelligence Summaries are contained in F. S. Regs., Part II. and the Staff Manual respectively. Title Pages will be prepared in manuscript.

WAR DIARY
or
~~INTELLIGENCE SUMMARY~~
(Erase heading not required.)

183 M. G. Co.

Army Form C. 2118.

Place	Date	Hour	Summary of Events and Information	Remarks and references to Appendices
In the Field	8/9/16	am 6.0	Front line guns carried out their usual programme. A working(?) party was fired on & dispersed at M 30 a 4. 4½	[initials]
	9/9/16		The last 24 hours have been fairly quiet except for occasional shelling of Moated Grange. A few shells fell near Winchester Post	
			There was practically no retaliation to our M.G. fire, nor was any noticed against our artillery.	[initials]
			Indirect Fire was directed on following targets with occasional bursts on surrounding country	
			1. N19 c 3 2 — N25 b 5 7	
			2 N25 a 1.2 — M30 d 8.7	
			3 N25 c 6.1 — N31 a 0 1½	
			Front line guns swept enemy's wire & parapet during night.	
	10/9/16		Indirect Fire was carried out last night against M30 a 7.3 – M 30 b 6. 8½ enemy front & support trenches in enfilade	[initials]

Instructions regarding War Diaries and Intelligence Summaries are contained in F. S. Regs., Part II. and the Staff Manual respectively. Title Pages will be prepared in manuscript.

WAR DIARY
or
~~INTELLIGENCE SUMMARY~~
(Erase heading not required.)

183 M.G. Co.

Army Form C. 2118.

Place	Date	Hour	Summary of Events and Information	Remarks and references to Appendices
In the Field	10/9/16		Indirect Fire against N25 b 4 2½ — N25. c 6 1.	
			There was the usual activity by front line guns but no enemy parties were observed or reported	
			Considerable enemy M.G. fire was noticed at various times particularly in the vicinity of one of our I.F. positions.	[initials]
			It was totally ineffective as far as our guns were concerned.	
			Enemy Artillery was very quiet	
	11/9/16		This company ~~[struck out]~~ packed up all material and was relieved in the Moated Grange Sector by 184 M.G. Co.	[initials]
			The company then marched to Lestrem and took over billets previously occupied by 184 M.G. Co. at R2c 9 8 and R2d 7 8 (transport & 1 Section).	
	12/9/16		Holiday according to Orders received	[initials]

2449 Wt. W14957/M90 750,000 1/16 J.B.C. & A. Forms/C.2118/12.

Instructions regarding War Diaries and Intelligence Summaries are contained in F. S. Regs., Part II. and the Staff Manual respectively. Title Pages will be prepared in manuscript.

WAR DIARY

or

~~INTELLIGENCE SUMMARY~~

(Erase heading not required.)

Army Form C. 2118.

183 MG Co

Place	Date	Hour	Summary of Events and Information	Remarks and references to Appendices
In the Field	13/9/16	7.0 am 7.30	Physical Training	
		9 am 11.0	Cleaning and Packing Limbers	
		11.15 to 12.15	Gas Helmet & Kit Inspection	[illegible]
		12.15 to 12.45	Lecture for Sections by Section Officers	
	14/9/16	7.0 am to 7.30	Physical Training	
		9.0 am 10.0	Infantry Drill	
		10.0 am 11.0	Stoppages	[illegible]
		11.15 to 12.15	Rifle Manual	
		12.15 12.45	Lecture	
	15/9/16.	7.0 to 7.30 am	Physical Training	[illegible]
		9.0 to 11.0	Action from Limbers	
		11.30 to 12.30	Mechanism & Stoppages	
			During day Neuve Chapelle, ~~[illegible]~~ sector north of La Bassee Rd held by 93 MG Co was reconnoitred.	

2449 Wt. W14957/M90 750,000 1/16 J.B.C. & A. Forms/C.2118/12.

Instructions regarding War Diaries and Intelligence Summaries are contained in F. S. Regs., Part II. and the Staff Manual respectively. Title Pages will be prepared in manuscript.

WAR DIARY
or
~~INTELLIGENCE~~ SUMMARY
(Erase heading not required.)

183 MG Co

Army Form C. 2118.

Place	Date	Hour	Summary of Events and Information	Remarks and references to Appendices
In the Field	16/9/16		During the day positions were taken over from 93 MG Co at :- Front Line No 9, 10, 3. Posts. Port Arthur, neuve Chappelle, Brickfields, Oxford Post. Port Loggy, + Euston	
			During the night front line guns kept enemy front line and were under fire	[initials]
		pm 8.45	An enemy MG at about S11 a 6.3. fired on + silenced	
		10.15 pm	Working party at A11 a 5.3 was dispersed + casualties inflicted.	
		am 12.0 to 4.0	Our working parties were operating	
		3.30 am	Enemy party fired on and dispersed S5 b 7½. 8	
			MG. 3 emplacement is in a most delapidated condition and considered quite unfit for occupation. An enemy ~~minne~~ minnewerfer which wrecked the next bay this morning nearly shook it down. It requires much R.E. attention.	
	17/9/16		The whole day and night have been comparatively quiet	[initials]

2449 Wt. W14957/M90 750,000 1/16 J.B.C. & A. Forms/C.2118/12.

Instructions regarding War Diaries and Intelligence Summaries are contained in F. S. Regs., Part II. and the Staff Manual respectively. Title pages will be prepared in manuscript.

WAR DIARY
or
~~INTELLIGENCE SUMMARY~~.
(Erase heading not required.)

183 M G Co.

Army Form C. 2118.

Place	Date	Hour	Summary of Events and Information	Remarks and references to Appendices
In the Field	17/9/16		Indirect Fire was carried out against La Tourelle and on a line S17 a 8.6 - S11 a 8.3. & communications short of the Front line guns fired as usual	
		pm 4.30	Working party was dispersed at M36c 1 5½ & other enemy parties were effectively fired on at S11a 5.4. At this point a party appeared to be persistant as they came out 2 or 3 times.	
			An enemy gun at S11a 6.3 ceased firing on our opening fire at him.	
			Work has been done at Oxford. The barrier of sandbags obstructing field of fire of right loophole has been cut through and a screen of wire and sandbags has been erected over the breach.	[initials]
			At Port Arthur an open emplacement in the trench has been constructed & a new dugout has been started on	

2353 Wt. W2544/1454 700,000 5/15 D. D. & L. A.D.S.S./Forms/C. 2118.

Instructions regarding War Diaries and Intelligence Summaries are contained in F. S. Regs., Part II. and the Staff Manual respectively. Title pages will be prepared in manuscript.

WAR DIARY
or
~~INTELLIGENCE SUMMARY.~~
(Erase heading not required.)

Army Form C. 2118.

183 M.G.Co.

Place	Date	Hour	Summary of Events and Information	Remarks and references to Appendices
In the Field	18/9/16		The day was quiet except for a slight retaliation to our T.M. fire	
			Enemy M.Gs were active at night.	
		8pm 30 to 12.30	Indirect Fire against S11 c 5.4 & S11 d. 3.0.	[illegible]
			Front line guns fired as usual	
			Enemy working parties ceased operations under our fire at M 36 c 1 5½ S11 b 7.5 & S11 a 9.7	
	19/9/16.		The day was fairly quiet, only the usual desultory shelling being noticed.	
		5.0pm	Indirect Fire was carried out by 2 guns against S5d 3.0 – S6a. 3.0 enfilading front line & enemy communication in S6a.	[illegible]
		9.0pm to 11.30pm	Indirect Fire targets were { S11 b 3.0 to S11 d 9.4	
			Breaches in parapet made during the afternoon at about S5 b 8.5 & M 35 d 9.2 were kept under fire during night by front line guns.	

2353 Wt. W2544/1454 700,000 5/15 D. D. & L. A.D.S.S./Forms/C. 2118.

Instructions regarding War Diaries and Intelligence Summaries are contained in F. S. Regs., Part II. and the Staff Manual respectively. Title pages will be prepared in manuscript.

WAR DIARY
or
~~INTELLIGENCE~~ SUMMARY.
(Erase heading not required.)

183 MGCoy

Army Form C. 2118.

Place	Date	Hour	Summary of Events and Information	Remarks and references to Appendices
In the Field	19/9/16		Working parties were fired on & dispersed at S11a 8 5 & S11 a 53 Enemy front line & wire was kept under fire all night Work is being done at Oxford Post and it is expected to have an additional cellar made habitable shortly.	[illegible]
	20/9/16		The day was quiet except for TM fire and a vigorous bombardment away to our left at 10.0 pm. Indirect Fire was carried out against line S11 b 2 2 – S11 b 8 6 A fresh gap at about M35 d. 8¾ 2¾ in the enemy parapet was kept under fire from our front line guns, and also 2 made the day before Working parties at M36 C7.3. S11 a 5.3 were dispersed by our fire.	[illegible]

2353 Wt. W2544/1454 700,000 5/15 D. D. & L. A.D.S.S./Forms/C. 2118.

Instructions regarding War Diaries and Intelligence Summaries are contained in F. S. Regs., Part II. and the Staff Manual respectively. Title pages will be prepared in manuscript.

WAR DIARY
or
INTELLIGENCE SUMMARY.
(Erase heading not required.)

Army Form C. 2118.

183 M. G. Coy.

Place	Date	Hour	Summary of Events and Information	Remarks and references to Appendices
In the Field	21/9/16		Enemy artillery active during late afternoon & about 9pm Indirect Fire against enemy front line and supports A11d and against line A6c.07 – A6a 6.4, in connection with a TM shoot at 4.0 to 6pm Front line guns fired as usual At A11a 5.3 a working party was dispersed with accurate fire Casualties were observed Fire in conjunction with Infantry Plans was also carried out & gaps in enemy parapet were kept continuously under fire with short bursts all night Necessary repairs to MGE 3 & plans for dugout at Port Arthur were arranged with RE. Oxford Post drained, cellar cleared out, & thoroughly disinfected.	[initials]
	22/9/16		The day was fairly quiet but between 2.0 & 3.0 am a number of enemy Minnewerfer came over.	[initials]

2353 Wt. W2544/1454 700,000 5/15 D. D. & L. A.D.S.S./Forms/C. 2118.

Instructions regarding War Diaries and Intelligence Summaries are contained in F. S. Regs., Part II. and the Staff Manual respectively. Title pages will be prepared in manuscript.

WAR DIARY
or
~~INTELLIGENCE SUMMARY.~~
(Erase heading not required.)

183 MGCo.

Army Form C. 2118.

Place	Date	Hour	Summary of Events and Information	Remarks and references to Appendices
In the Field	22/9/16		In conjunction with TM programme I.F. was fired at 3.0, 5.0, 7.0pm against area S6a 5.2 – S6d 3.7 – S6d 5.9 – S6a 6.3 + line S6a 9.8 – S6a 6.4	
		9pm	Against La Bassee Rd S11c 5.4 to La Tourelle crossroads	
			Front line guns did their usual work + gave liberal attention to gaps in enemy parapet.	
			An enemy mg at S5b 7.3 was fired on, it ceased fire almost at once + did not reopen from this position.	[initials]
			An enemy party was fired on with good effect at M35d83 It is thought these people were engaged in repair work	
			Work was continued at Port Arthur on new dugout	
	22/9/16.		Front line guns firing as usual. caught two working parties in gaps about M35d 8 2. on both occasions.	
			Indirect Fire was carried out against enemy's works around S6c 9.3 + the tramway through ~~here~~ was occasionally searched. Tracks on the south side of Bois du Biez were also searched + traversing SE corner	[initials]

2353 Wt. W2544/1454 700,000 5/15 D. D. & L. A.D.S.S./Forms/C. 2118.

Instructions regarding War Diaries and Intelligence Summaries are contained in F. S. Regs., Part II. and the Staff Manual respectively. Title pages will be prepared in manuscript.

WAR DIARY

or

~~INTELLIGENCE SUMMARY.~~

(Erase heading not required.)

183 MG Co.

Army Form C. 2118.

Place	Date	Hour	Summary of Events and Information	Remarks and references to Appendices
In the Field	23/9/16.		The day was normal with some ~~[illegible]~~ shelling from both sides.	
	24/9/16.		Except for a few MG items the day and night were fairly quiet on this sector.	
	~~Dusk & 4.45~~	Dusk & 9.45	Gaps S5b7½ 9½ & S5a 2.4 were fired on also again from 130 am to 1.45 am & 3.0 – 3.15 am	
		1.00 pm	Infantry reported raiding party about S5b5.2 This direction was swept with swinging traverse & nothing happened no one was seen by us. A working party observed in parapet S5b7.8 was fired on & dispersed at 12.45 am. Occasional bursts of fire were directed along the whole of enemy front line, & an enemy working party about S11a4.4 was dispersed	[initials]
	25/9/16	3.00 pm 4.30	Indirect fire was applied against enemy front & support trenches in rear of road S5d 3½ 1 – S5d 4½ 3. On each occasion after a 15 mins pause we gave them an extra belt.	[initials]

2353 Wt. W2544/1454 700,000 5/15 D. D. & L. A.D.S.S./Forms/C. 2118.

Instructions regarding War Diaries and Intelligence Summaries are contained in F. S. Regs., Part II. and the Staff Manual respectively. Title pages will be prepared in manuscript.

WAR DIARY
or
~~INTELLIGENCE~~ SUMMARY.
(Erase heading not required.)

183 MG Co.

Army Form C. 2118.

Place	Date	Hour	Summary of Events and Information	Remarks and references to Appendices
In the Field.	25/9/16	10pm	We again used Indirect Fire to search ~~communication~~ [lines] N & S. of the Bois du Biez	
		11.15 pm	Fired 2 belts rapid at work at rear of road S6a 3 1 – S6a 9½ 9 Considerable enemy Indirect Fire fell along Rue Tilleloy & La Bassee Rd at this time.	
			In the Front line enemy wire & parapet was fired on as usual and one gun was held in readiness to support our raiding party	
		11.30 pm	Fire from this gun was opened to a flank, & on the return of our party we searched No Mans Land & swept enemy wire & parapet towards M35 d 9.3 The Infantry had reported the Hun following him back & it is hoped this report was true	
		2.10 am	Enemy patrol was reported at M35 d 9.4 This was immediately fired on & good ~~rep~~ Results reported. Enemy MGs in front line were active.	
	26/9/16		They day was quiet except for the usual retaliation to our TM fire	
		4.30 pm & 6.0 pm	Indirect Fire against line of communication S17a 9.6. – S11 d 8.3	

2353 Wt. W2544/1454 700,000 5/15 D. D. & L. A.D.S.S./Forms/C. 2118.

Instructions regarding War Diaries and Intelligence Summaries are contained in F. S. Regs., Part II. and the Staff Manual respectively. Title pages will be prepared in manuscript.

WAR DIARY
or
~~INTELLIGENCE SUMMARY~~.
(Erase heading not required.)

183 MGCo.

Army Form C. 2118.

Place	Date	Hour	Summary of Events and Information	Remarks and references to Appendices
In the Field	26/9/16	10.0pm	Fme du Bois (S12c12½) + vicinity was swept with fire by one gun. + the road S12c½½ – S12c7.5 was swept by a second gun.	
			Considerable enemy MG fire was noticed in reply.	
			Front line guns fired as usual + enemy parties were fired on at S5d2.4. (apparently wiring) + M35d8.3	[initials]
			An enemy MG firing about S5b7.3 was fired on and silenced.	
		am 12.30	Fire directed against S6a5.1, the sound of moving trucks on the tramway at once ceased.	
	27/9/16		The usual reply to our TM fire was the only noteworthy point in an otherwise quiet day	
			Front line guns fired as usual + an enemy patrol at M35d9.5 was fired on in the early hours of the morning.	
			MG's were observed firing at S5b7.3 & M35 9.4 on being fired on by our guns then ceased fire.	[initials]
		9.0 & 10.30pm	Indirect Fire in conjunction with other Operations ~~at~~ against Communications tect. S6a4.2 – S6d3.7 + S6a8½ – 7 – M36d7.8.	
	28/9/16.	12noon	Port Arthur shelled	[initials]

2353 Wt. W2544/1454 700,000 5/15 D. D. & L. A.D.S.S./Forms/C. 2118.

Army Form C. 2118.

WAR DIARY
or
~~INTELLIGENCE SUMMARY~~.
(*Erase heading not required.*)

183 M G Co.

Instructions regarding War Diaries and Intelligence Summaries are contained in F. S. Regs., Part II. and the Staff Manual respectively. Title pages will be prepared in manuscript.

Place	Date	Hour	Summary of Events and Information	Remarks and references to Appendices
In the Field	28/9/16		Indirect fire was applied to Pietre cross roads N31 a ½ 2½ also against La Russe & traversing the line S6a 5-9 - S6c 8½. Front line guns fired as usual & at 12.30pm an enemy party was caught in the open at S11 a 4 4½	[initials]
	29/9/16		Our artillery was somewhat active and the enemy reply was not considerable although he managed to do some damage to Chateau Rd	
		8.0am	6 dummies were exposed in the enemy parapet opposite MG E9 As the Hun had sent C Shells over in this direction during the night it is thought possible that he was making an attempt to draw fire and confirm certain suspicions. There was however ~~nothing~~ no result. During the night our front line guns followed their usual programme & kept the enemy lines under fire. On the right their activity was limited by the Infantry operations	[initials]

2353 Wt. W2544/1454 700,000 5/15 D. D. & L. A.D.S.S./Forms/C. 2118.

WAR DIARY
or
~~INTELLIGENCE SUMMARY.~~
(Erase heading not required.)

183 M.G.Co

Army Form C. 2118.

Instructions regarding War Diaries and Intelligence Summaries are contained in F. S. Regs., Part II. and the Staff Manual respectively. Title pages will be prepared in manuscript.

Place	Date	Hour	Summary of Events and Information	Remarks and references to Appendices
In the Field	29/9/16		An enemy party was observed & fired on at S11a4 4½. Parties are often seen here.	
			At S5b7½ 8½ another enemy party was fired on effectively & from near the bottom of Church Rd the enemy's front & support lines were enfiladed.	[illegible]
		3.10 3.50	Indirect Fire in conjunction with TM programme was carried out against Ligny le petit & La Tourelle Rd	
		5.50 pm [illegible]	Indirect Fire against La Tourelle Rd Ligny le Petit & Fme du Becq. From the reply it is thought this was effective. The walls of the Chateau are becoming unsafe. The front is crumbling & the side walls are getting a list on. If these walls fall the emplacement here will show up most ~~[illegible]~~ conspicuously, & is almost certain to be demolished.	
	30/9/16		Our artillery were active during the day & retaliation was forthcoming on the front line & Chateau Rd.	[illegible]

2353 Wt. W2544/1454 700,000 5/15 D. D. & L. A.D.S.S./Forms/C. 2118.

Army Form C. 2118.

WAR DIARY
or
~~INTELLIGENCE SUMMARY~~. 183 M G Co.

(Erase heading not required.)

Instructions regarding War Diaries and Intelligence Summaries are contained in F. S. Regs., Part II. and the Staff Manual respectively. Title pages will be prepared in manuscript.

Place	Date	Hour	Summary of Events and Information	Remarks and references to Appendices
In the Field	30/9/16.		Front line guns did the usual work against enemy front line & a working party was caught at S5 b 7 3/4 6 3/4.	
		8.0 pm	Indirect fire against front & support lines at Les Brulot; this was stopped at 9.0 pm at the request of the Infantry.	
		9.0 pm 1.30 am	Indirect was also applied sweeping the enemy communication from H1 Pommereau to the La Bassee Rd at ranges from 2000–3000 yds.	[illegible]
			Dickering D. Perry Lt. 2nd in Com. 183 M. G. Coy.	
			1.10.16.	

183 Inf. Bde

183rd. Bde M.G. Coy

War Diary for October 1916

Vol 5

Instructions regarding War Diaries and Intelligence Summaries are contained in F. S. Regs., Part II. and the Staff Manual respectively. Title pages will be prepared in manuscript.

WAR DIARY
or
~~INTELLIGENCE SUMMARY.~~ 183 MGCo.

(Erase heading not required.)

Army Form C. 2118.

Place	Date	Hour	Summary of Events and Information	Remarks and references to Appendices
In the Field	1/10/16		The front line has been much damaged by enemy fire & the parapet is breached in the vicinity of Chateau Trench	[initials]
		7.0pm	Pont Logy was shelled with H.E. for 3/4 of an hour. Several hits were registered & the walls have been knocked about considerably	
			Front line guns fired as usual on enemy front line & parapet.	
		9.0 9.15 10.15 10.30	Communications in M36d & S6a & Ligny le petit came under our Indirect Fire.	
	2/10/16		Chateau trench was again a enemy target and it is now ~~it is~~ in almost an impassible state. There was also some TM firing on the front line of the right sector. Indirect Fire was applied to Ht Pommereau communication in the rear of the Bois du Biez	

2353 Wt. W2544/1454 700,000 5/15 D. D. & L. A.D.S.S./Forms/C. 2118.

Instructions regarding War Diaries and Intelligence Summaries are contained in F. S. Regs., Part II. and the Staff Manual respectively. Title pages will be prepared in manuscript.

WAR DIARY
or
~~INTELLIGENCE SUMMARY.~~ 183 MG Co

(*Erase heading not required.*)

Army Form C. 2118.

Place	Date	Hour	Summary of Events and Information	Remarks and references to Appendices
In the Field	2/10/16		and road in M36a + S6a, These targets were fired on for 10 mins at 5.30, 6.0, + 6.30pm in conjunction with TM programme.	
			Front line guns fired as usual on enemys front line + wire but no working parties were observed or reported.	HP
	3/10/16		There was not the usual retaliation on Chateau, to our artillery + TM shoot, but Oxford + Port Arthur were fired on between 4.10 pm + 5.0 pm, + the front line MG E3 came in for attention	
		8.30pm 10.30pm (during night)	Ligny le petit + vicinity, "Seven sisters" + communications in Bois du Biez were fired on.	
			A working party at S5 b 8.5 was caught by one of our front line guns; firing of the usual programme was carried out.	HP
	4/9/16		A company internal relief was completed by 11.30 am	

Army Form C. 2118.

Instructions regarding War Diaries and Intelligence Summaries are contained in F. S. Regs., Part II. and the Staff Manual respectively. Title pages will be prepared in manuscript.

WAR DIARY
or
~~INTELLIGENCE SUMMARY.~~ 183 M.G.Coy

(Erase heading not required.)

Place	Date	Hour	Summary of Events and Information	Remarks and references to Appendices
In the Field	4/9/16		The day & night were unusually quiet; at night the enemy used very few Very lights.	
			Front line guns fired intermittently during the night on enemy parapet & wire. No parties were observed or reported.	[illegible]
	5/9/16		The day was fairly quiet & there was not so much retaliation to the afternoon shoot as usual.	
			Indirect fire was carried out in accordance with programme during the night against communication in S11d, & S12c	
			Front line guns fired as usual	
		8.30pm	An enemy party were ~~attacked~~ reported working in a sap S5b 7.5 Fire was opened on them & cries were heard. The enemy also opened fire with a machine gun in reply & sent up 5 green lights.	[illegible]
	6/9/16		There was no usual artillery activity during the day & the night was very quiet.	
			Indirect fire was applied to Ht Pommereau road M36 d ½ 0 – M36 a 8.9½	

2353 Wt. W2544/1454 700,000 5/15 D. D. & L. A.D.S.S./Forms/C. 2118.

Instructions regarding War Diaries and Intelligence Summaries are contained in F. S. Regs., Part II. and the Staff Manual respectively. Title pages will be prepared in manuscript.

WAR DIARY
or
~~INTELLIGENCE SUMMARY.~~
(Erase heading not required.)

183 MGCo

Army Form C. 2118.

Place	Date	Hour	Summary of Events and Information	Remarks and references to Appendices
In the Field	6/10/16		continued Oct 6th in conjunction with TM programme Front line guns fired as usual, but no enemy activity was in evidence.	[illegible]
	7/10/16		The day was normal with some enemy shelling, he apparently searched for a battery thought to be near Pont Logy, with shrapnel, but had no success. Indirect fire was carried out as per programme against Ht Pommereau S11 d 5.9½ – S11 d 9.3 + S11 b 8 3½ S12a 4.0. During a burst against Ht Pommereau a small party of Germans was seen to hurriedly take cover. At night communication in S6a were searched with fire. Front line guns fired as usual. On the left one gun stood by to support an infantry bombing ~~[illegible]~~ party who attempted to enter the enemy trenches. Nothing happened. ~~[illegible]~~	

2353 Wt. W2544/1454 700,000 5/15 D. D. & L. A.D.S.S./Forms/C. 2118.

Army Form C. 2118.

Instructions regarding War Diaries and Intelligence Summaries are contained in F. S. Regs., Part II. and the Staff Manual respectively. Title pages will be prepared in manuscript.

WAR DIARY
or
~~INTELLIGENCE SUMMARY.~~ 183 M G Co

(*Erase heading not required.*)

Place	Date	Hour	Summary of Events and Information	Remarks and references to Appendices
			continued Oct 7th	
In the Field	7/10/16		and only one German was seen by the party which returned	[illegible]
	8/10/16		Indirect fire was carried out in conjunction with TM programme against communication in S6a + M36d + also during the night.	
			Fire was again opened on Ht Pommereau + this was sure to disconcert the enemy parties passing along the road. These men immediately took cover until the bursts ceased.	
			Front line guns fired as usual + two enemy M Gs were engaged during the night on every occasion they ceased fire when we opened.	[illegible]
	9/10/16		Indirect Fire was carried out against Ht Pommereau + N flank of Bois du Biez.	
			Front line guns fired as usual. An enemy M G covering a working party was fired on + silenced + the party dispersed S5C 8 7.	

2353 Wt. W2544/1454 700,000 5/15 D. D. & L. A.D.S.S./Forms/C. 2118.

Instructions regarding War Diaries and Intelligence Summaries are contained in F. S. Regs., Part II. and the Staff Manual respectively. Title pages will be prepared in manuscript.

WAR DIARY

or

~~INTELLIGENCE SUMMARY.~~

(Erase heading not required.)

183 M G Co

Army Form C. 2118.

Place	Date	Hour	Summary of Events and Information	Remarks and references to Appendices
In the Field	9/10/16	12 mn	An enemy M.G. firing on one of our working parties was engaged & silenced so that our people were able to continue.	
			An enemy party was reported by infantry at S5 b 8.9. Fire was opened & the party were reported to have disappeared.	[initials]
	10/10/16		Little artillery activity was noticed	
		6.30 pm	4 H.Es were put into Chateau Redoubt	
			In cooperation with our raiding party our front line guns silenced an enemy M.G. that opened from Les Brulots. The gun which held up our party could not be engaged owing to our fire being masked by our own men.	
			No attempt appeared to be made to get this gun under. It fired remarkably few rounds, but very accurately. Six guns laid for a barrage were not called upon.	

2353 Wt. W2544/1454 700,000 5/15 D. D. & L. A.D.S.S./Forms/C. 2118.

Army Form C. 2118.

Instructions regarding War Diaries and Intelligence Summaries are contained in F. S. Regs., Part II. and the Staff Manual respectively. Title pages will be prepared in manuscript.

WAR DIARY
or
INTELLIGENCE SUMMARY.
(Erase heading not required.)

Place	Date	Hour	Summary of Events and Information	Remarks and references to Appendices
In the Field	10/10/16		On the left our front line guns kept enemy front line under fire at intervals throughout the night.	[initials]
	11/10/16		The day was quiet & no activity was noticed on the enemy side.	
			Two parties of 8 germans were seen filling up the road near Ht Pommereau	
			Indirect fire was carried out against Halpegarbe between 9.0 pm & 1.0 am.	
			Front line guns fired as usual at intervals during the night. No enemy parties were reported or observed.	[initials]
	12/10/16		There was an increase in enemy artillery activity during the day. Support works in front of B Line on the left were shelled & forward of Pont Logy N.	
			Front line guns fired as usual but the enemy's front line was quiet.	

2353 Wt. W2544/1454 700,000 5/15 D. D. & L. A.D.S.S./Forms/C. 2118.

Instructions regarding War Diaries and Intelligence Summaries are contained in F. S. Regs., Part II. and the Staff Manual respectively. Title pages will be prepared in manuscript.

WAR DIARY
or
~~INTELLIGENCE~~ SUMMARY.
(Erase heading not required.)

Army Form C. 2118.

183 MG Co.

Place	Date	Hour	Summary of Events and Information	Remarks and references to Appendices
In the Field	12/10/16	30am	On the right he bombed his own wire.	
			Indirect fire was carried out in the afternoon as per programme against CTs in S11c + S6a + also at right, on S12c23 + CTs in S11d + the Bois du Biez also against S23 b 8½ 3 this latter point is thought to be a dump + was under observation from Factory OP	MB.
	13/10/16		Enemy shelled short of Pont Logy N in the afternoon + in the morning put 10 light shells into the front line to the right of MGE 3 6 of which were blind	
			Indirect Fire under observation from Curzon Post carried out again + after the first burst all passage along the road near Het Pommereau was stopped + two Germans were seen to be stationed at 2 points + signalled to each other in semaphore.	
			Indirect Fire was also carried out in accordance with	

2353 Wt. W2544/1454 700,000 5/15 D. D. & L. A.D.S.S./Forms/C. 2118.

Instructions regarding War Diaries and Intelligence Summaries are contained in F. S. Regs., Part II. and the Staff Manual respectively. Title pages will be prepared in manuscript.

WAR DIARY
or
~~INTELLIGENCE SUMMARY.~~
(Erase heading not required.)

Army Form C. 2118.

183 M.G.Co.

Place	Date	Hour	Summary of Events and Information	Remarks and references to Appendices
In the Field	13/10/16		continued programme against S11a central & Ligny lepetit this was continued during the night & IF from our right was also applied to ~~ca~~ La Tourelle cross roads & S23 b7.4 (suspected dump) During these operations a few light shells fell near the Copse position. Front line guns fired as usual no enemy activity was observed or reported.	MP
	14/10/16		During the day the enemy activity was very slight and there was little retaliation to the afternoon shoot but at 10.30 he sent over a number of minnies & HEs. Indirect fire was carried out as per programme against S11 central and Ligny lepetit, this was continued during the night and also fire was applied to the La Tourelle cross roads and a suspected dump at S23 b7.4. Front line guns fired as usual at enemy parapet & wire but no special activity was reported.	MP

2353 Wt. W2544/1454 700,000 5/15 D. D. & L. A.D.S.S./Forms/C. 2118.

Instructions regarding War Diaries and Intelligence Summaries are contained in F. S. Regs., Part II. and the Staff Manual respectively. Title pages will be prepared in manuscript.

WAR DIARY
or
~~INTELLIGENCE SUMMARY.~~
(*Erase heading not required.*)

183 MGC

Army Form C. 2118.

Place	Date	Hour	Summary of Events and Information	Remarks and references to Appendices
In the Field	15/10/16		Enemy shelled close to the orchard near Rue Tilleloy close to I F position between 2pm + 4pm and shelled Sign Post at 7.30pm but did not retaliate to our shelling and Trench Mortar Shoot. Indirect Fire was carried out as per programme at Roads + CTs in S12c Roads + CTs in M36d ~~Roads~~ CTs in S6a and at night at the Bois Du Biez and S11c An enemy dump was observed at S15c½ 1 and considerable movement was noted. This target was immediately put under fire and also at intervals during the night. Front line guns fired as usual during the night on the enemy wire and parapet. An enemy patrol was reported + fired on with success but otherwise no special activity was reported.	[initials]
	16/10/16		Front line guns in conjunction with patrols fired at gaps in enemy wire. Our gun mounted near No 3 MGE	

2353 Wt. W2544/1454 700,000 5/15 D. D. & L. A.D.S.S./Forms/C. 2118.

Instructions regarding War Diaries and Intelligence Summaries are contained in F. S. Regs., Part II. and the Staff Manual respectively. Title pages will be prepared in manuscript.

WAR DIARY
or
~~INTELLIGENCE SUMMARY.~~
(Erase heading not required.)

183 M.G. Co.

Army Form C. 2118.

Place	Date	Hour	Summary of Events and Information	Remarks and references to Appendices
In the Field	16/10/16		opened intense fire on hostile party who were endeavouring to repair the gap at S11a 4 3. Casualties were inflicted & the party were dispersed rapidly. No further attempts were made during the night to repair the wire.	
			Indirect Fire The guns fired indirect on the following targets Roads & CTs in S11d Roads & CTs in S6a at intervals from 7am to 8.00 am an average of 3,000 rds per gun was expended. Indirect fire was also brought to bear on Enemy Dump at S17c ½ 8½ fire was kept up in intermittent bursts during the day & night.	
			Hostile MG fire was only of a desultory nature. During the afternoon a hostile aeroplane flew over Edwards Post but was turned by our anti aircraft guns.	
			Indirect Fire Positions near the Rue Tilleloy improved for nights firing, Work is being ~~done~~ carried out during the day on new MG IFP at Hush Hall Transport lines & billets have been whitewashed.	HB

2353 Wt. W2544/1454 700,000 5/15 D. D. & L. A.D.S.S./Forms/C. 2118.

Instructions regarding War Diaries and Intelligence Summaries are contained in F. S. Regs., Part II. and the Staff Manual respectively. Title pages will be prepared in manuscript.

WAR DIARY
or
~~INTELLIGENCE SUMMARY~~.
(Erase heading not required.)

183 M G Co

Army Form C. 2118.

Place	Date	Hour	Summary of Events and Information	Remarks and references to Appendices
In the Field.	17/10/16	9pm	Guns in the front line near M G E 10 dispersed a hostile patrol which was observed at about M35 d 7 3 the ~~effect~~ night was too dark to observe if there were any casualties.	
		2:20pm & 8:40pm	4 Guns brought heavy fire to bear on the following targets CTs from S11c 8 3½ to S11 d 4.1 Southern edge of Bois du Biez Les Brulot & CTs in S11d. between the hours of 8'30p to 8'40pm our Machine gun fire was very intense. The roads & CT of the Bois du Biez also the neighbourhood of S11d were fired on during the whole of the night. 20,000 ~~Operat~~ rds were expended during the day & night firing. Port Arthur was nearly Shattered during the afternoon	
		8:30 8:45pm	The enemy replied to our TM fire with his Machine Gun fire A number of shells burst close to Windy Corner he also traversed between Edwards & the La Bassee Rd. evidently searching for our IFPs but without success.	MA

2353 Wt. W2544/1454 700,000 5/15 D. D. & L. A.D.S.S./Forms/C. 2118.

Army Form C. 2118.

Instructions regarding War Diaries and Intelligence Summaries are contained in F. S. Regs., Part II. and the Staff Manual respectively. Title pages will be prepared in manuscript.

WAR DIARY
or
~~INTELLIGENCE SUMMARY.~~ 183 M G Co
(Erase heading not required.)

Place	Date	Hour	Summary of Events and Information	Remarks and references to Appendices
In the Field	18/10/16		Both front line guns & guns laid for Indirect Fire were silent during last 24 hours	
		3·0 a – 4·0 p	A few shrapnel shells were fired at Copse Post, but enemy Machine Guns very quiet	
			M G Emplacements in Brigade Section were examined	[illegible]
			Work is being continued on IFP at Heush Hall.	

Instructions regarding War Diaries and Intelligence Summaries are contained in F. S. Regs., Part II. and the Staff Manual respectively. Title pages will be prepared in manuscript.

WAR DIARY
or
~~INTELLIGENCE SUMMARY.~~
(Erase heading not required.)

183 MG Co

Army Form C. 2118.

Place	Date	Hour	Summary of Events and Information	Remarks and references to Appendices
In the Field	19/10/16		Front line guns did not fire, no suitable target presenting itself.	
			3 guns fired Indirect Fire from Different IFPs at the following targets at intervals during the night. SW corner of Bois du Biez CTs in S11c (enfilade fire) CTs in S11d 3,000 rds per gun was expended.	
			A number of rifle grenades fell in the neighbourhood of No 9 MGE between the hours of 12.30 + 2.30 am. In the morning he shelled Windy Corner. At noon several HEs were dropped in the neighbourhood of Lansdowne Post + Edwards Post. At 9.30pm he searched for Chocolate + Oats Post	
			Work Done. Moving guns and ammunition to new position for IF, working at IFP at Hush Hall.	[illegible]
	20/10/16		2 of our front line guns were placed to protect flanks of the raiding party + to silence hostile machine gun fire being opened on raiding party. It was not found necessary to fire these guns	

2353 Wt. W2544/1454 700,000 5/15 D. D. & L. A.D.S.S. Forms/C. 2118.

Instructions regarding War Diaries and Intelligence Summaries are contained in F. S. Regs., Part II. and the Staff Manual respectively. Title pages will be prepared in manuscript.

WAR DIARY
or
~~INTELLIGENCE SUMMARY.~~ 183 M G Co

(Erase heading not required.)

Army Form C. 2118.

Place	Date	Hour	Summary of Events and Information	Remarks and references to Appendices
In the Field	20/10/16		Indirect Fire. A double barrage was formed in the rear of area raided. Shortly after zero a battery of 6 guns placed at Pont Logy opened intense fire on the following positions:- 1 gun searched & traversed SE corner of Bois du Biez. 2 Gun searched & traversed CTs in S11d. 3 Gun searched & traversed Ligny le Petit. 4 Gun searched CTs & road in S11a. 5 Gun fired on La Tourelle. 6 Gun S17a CTs & roads.	
			Lansdowne Post 1 FP Gun searched SW corner of Bois du Biez & Les Brulot. 1 Gun Cat Post 1 FP enfilading CTs in S11d. 1 Chocolate Post 1 FP enfiladed CTs in S11a.	
			Our gun fired 60,000 rds between the hours of 8.45 pm & 11.40 pm. German Machine gun did not retaliate on front line & their indirect fire was weak. At 9.30 pm our front line was heavily shelled ~~at~~ Lansdowne Post CT was shelled with Minenwerfer. In the morning Pont Logy was shelled with 4.2's several falling near gun position	[initials]

2353 Wt. W2544/1454 700,000 5/15 D. D. & L. A.D.S.S./Forms/C. 2118.

Instructions regarding War Diaries and Intelligence Summaries are contained in F. S. Regs., Part II. and the Staff Manual respectively. Title pages will be prepared in manuscript.

WAR DIARY
or
~~INTELLIGENCE SUMMARY~~. 183 M G Co

(Erase heading not required.)

Army Form C. 2118.

Place	Date	Hour	Summary of Events and Information	Remarks and references to Appendices
In the Field	20/10/16		Enemy retaliated on our other posts during the night with shells of light calibre. Hostile aeroplanes observed directing fire on Pont Logy & surroundings. Work done carrying ammunition & improving IFP's for the raid	MG
	21/10/16		Front line guns did not fire last night. One gun fired Indirect Fire from Pont Logy IFP at the following targets Road & Buildings to NW of the Bois du Biez. From Lansdowne IFP one gun fired CTs at SW corner of Bois du Biez. One gun at Edwards Post IFP enfiladed CTs and road in S11c. Hostile machine guns fired fairly heavy sweeping the neighbourhood of Pont Logy and Lansdowne Post	
		9 pm	A patrol of Oxford & Bucks captured a German Prisoner on our left. He was slightly in advance of the patrol he was leading. Lansdowne IFP has been improved. Night firing emplacement at Hush Hall has been completed.	MG

2353 Wt. W2544/1454 700,000 5/15 D. D. & L. A.D.S.S. Forms/C 2118.

Army Form C. 2118.

Instructions regarding War Diaries and Intelligence Summaries are contained in F. S. Regs., Part II. and the Staff Manual respectively. Title pages will be prepared in manuscript.

WAR DIARY
or
~~INTELLIGENCE SUMMARY~~. 183 M G Co

(Erase heading not required.)

Place	Date	Hour	Summary of Events and Information	Remarks and references to Appendices
In the Field	22/10/16		Front line guns did not fire last night, no target presenting itself. Indirect Fire was carried out as per programme. Roads & CTs in S11 b Roads & CTs in S17 a Distillery in S17 c Roads & CTs in S6 a (North edge of Bois du Biez) and at intervals during the night. Enemy MG's quiet during day & night. New IFP at Lansdowne Post, dugout at Edwards Post improved and strengthened	[initials]
	23/10/16		Front line guns did not fire last night. Indirect Fire was applied on Roads & CTs in S6 a Roads & CTs in S12 c Roads & CTs in S17 a at intervals during the night. 3,000 rds per gun were fired. Hostile MG fire rather severe in the early part of the night searching for our Indirect Fire positions. Inter company relief carried out & IF positions improved	[initials]
	24/10/16		Front line guns fired 2000 rds. on enemy wire & parapet between 9.50 pm and 11.0 pm	

2353 Wt. W2544/1454 700,000 5/15 D. D. & L. A.D.S.S. Forms/C. 2118.

Instructions regarding War Diaries and Intelligence Summaries are contained in F. S. Regs., Part II. and the Staff Manual respectively. Title pages will be prepared in manuscript.

WAR DIARY
or
~~INTELLIGENCE SUMMARY~~.
(Erase heading not required.)

183 MGCo.

Army Form C. 2118.

Place	Date	Hour	Summary of Events and Information	Remarks and references to Appendices
In the Field	24/10/16		Indirect Fire. Lansdowne Post 1 gun fired on front line + supports in S5b 9½ 3 to S5b 9 8½ Edwards Post Target Front line + supports in S5b 9. 8 to M36c 2½ 3½ Port Lazy (right) 2 guns. Target Cross roads in S6a 6.4. to S6a 9½ 9 Target Running from S6a 3.1 to S6a 7 6. Rue Tilleloy (2 guns) Targets M36a 3½ 1 to M36a 8½ 1 + 1 gun C.T in M36 c 5 1½ to S6a 8.9. Those guns fired from 8.45 pm to 9.45 pm firing 2,000 rds each Operations of Enemy troops. Enemy's retaliation was ~~[illegible]~~ feeble Indirect fire positions + dugouts improved	[initials]
	25/10/16		Our front line guns did not fire last night Indirect Fire Roads + CTs in S6a Rds + CTs in S11d Rds + CTs in S17a. 2,000 rds per gun were fired. Enemy were quiet during day + night. Work Done Trench Draining + improving Oxford CT	[initials]

2353 Wt. W2544/1454 700,000 5/15 D. D. & L. A.D.S.S. Forms/C. 2118.

Instructions regarding War Diaries and Intelligence Summaries are contained in F. S. Regs., Part II. and the Staff Manual respectively. Title pages will be prepared in manuscript.

WAR DIARY
or
~~INTELLIGENCE SUMMARY~~. 183 M.G.Co

(Erase heading not required.)

Army Form C. 2118.

Place	Date	Hour	Summary of Events and Information	Remarks and references to Appendices
In the Field	26/10/16		Front line gun did not fire last night.	
			Indirect Fire was opened on Cross Roads & CTs in S17a Roads & CTs in S12a Road & CTs in S6a	
			2000 rds per gun were fired	
		7am to 8am	A number of Minnies and Air torpedoes fell to No 9 M.G. Emplacement but no damage was done. There was some artillery activity early this morning	
			Work was done on Trench Draining and general improvements	[initials]
	27/10/16		During the morning this company was relieved in its entirety by 169 M.G.Co who took over the sector occupied by us. Limbers were packed & the company minus those who remained behind ~~[illegible]~~ with 169 M.G.Co for instructional purposes marched to La Epinette, - Lestrem and billeted at Q12d05.	[initials]
	28/10/16		Billets cleaned, rifles cleaned and inspected also revolvers	

2353 Wt. W2544/1454 700,000 5/15 D. D. & L. A.D.S.S. Forms/C. 2118.

Instructions regarding War Diaries and Intelligence Summaries are contained in F. S. Regs., Part II. and the Staff Manual respectively. Title pages will be prepared in manuscript.

WAR DIARY
or
~~INTELLIGENCE SUMMARY.~~
(Erase heading not required.)

183 M.G.Co

Army Form C. 2118.

Place	Date	Hour	Summary of Events and Information	Remarks and references to Appendices
In the Field	28/10/16	2.0 pm	Men were paraded ~~with~~ in clean fatigue dress, & limbers overhauled together with guns & material & limbers repacked. Men who were left with 169 M.G.Co rejoined their company in the evening.	M.B.
	29/10/16	9.0 am	Company paraded & marched to Belle Rive – Gonnehem & were billeted in area V5 & 6 & proceeded to make billets habitable, latrines dug etc	M.B.
	30/10/16	8.0 am 8.30	Physical Training	
		8.30 to 9.0	Mechanism 9.0 am to 10 am Stoppages	
		10.15 11.15	Immediate Action 11.15 – 12. Lecture	
	31/10/16	8.0 to 8.30	Physical Training 8.30 am – 9.0 am Overhauling and Final Inspection of Guns	M.B.
		9.0 to 10.0 am	Revolver Cleaning & Practice for Nos 1 & 2 on gun Actions of Gun for Attached Men. Observation work for rest of company	
		10.05 11.15 am	Packing Limbers 11.15 to 12.15 Rapid Construction of MG Emplacements	

M. Betz Gerald Lt
OC 183 M G Coy

2353 Wt. W2544/1454 700,000 5/15 D. D. & L. A.D.S.S. Forms/C. 2118.

Vol 6

War Diary

– of –

183 Machine Gun Company

– for –

November 1916

Instructions regarding War Diaries and Intelligence Summaries are contained in F. S. Regs., Part II. and the Staff Manual respectively. Title pages will be prepared in manuscript.

WAR DIARY
or
INTELLIGENCE SUMMARY. 183 M.G.Co.
(Erase heading not required.)

Army Form C. 2118.

Place	Date	Hour	Summary of Events and Information	Remarks and references to Appendices
In the Field	1/11/16		The company paraded & marched to Auchel arriving there at 11·25 am & took up billets.	[illegible]
	2/11/16		Company paraded at 8am & at 8·30 am took ~~the~~ position in Brigade line of march & arrived at Houvelin at 3·25pm & billeted there	[illegible]
	3/11/16		Marched from Houvelin via Frévillers to le Tirlet & proceeded to make billets habitable	[illegible]
	4/11/16	8.50 to 10am	~~General~~ Parades thus:- General Description & Mechanism	
		10.15 to 11am	Overhauling guns & equipment.	
		11.15am to 12.15pm	Indication & recognition of targets.	[illegible]
		1.45pm to 2.45pm	Physical Training & NCOs Map reading	
		3 to 4pm	Gun Drill	
	5/11/16	9.35am	Company paraded full marching order, limbers packed ready to move off	[illegible]
		9.45am	Marched off and arrived at Foufflin Ricametz at 2 o'clock	

2353 Wt. W2544/1454 700,000 5/15 D. D. & L. A.D.S.S. Forms/C 2118

Instructions regarding War Diaries and Intelligence Summaries are contained in F. S. Regs., Part II. and the Staff Manual respectively. Title pages will be prepared in manuscript.

WAR DIARY
or
~~INTELLIGENCE SUMMARY.~~
(Erase heading not required.)

183 MGCo

Army Form C. 2118.

Place	Date	Hour	Summary of Events and Information	Remarks and references to Appendices
In the Field.	6/11/16	am 8.40	Paraded & marched company, met Brigade & took up position in line of march & arrived at Wavans at 4.25pm Stores, etc unpacked.	[initials]
	7/11/16		Parades as under:-	
		8.55am 9.45am	Mechanism and Stoppages.	
		9.55 11.0am	Concealment	[initials]
		11.10 12.15	Overhauling limbered wagons	
		1.50 to 4pm	Firing Vickers guns on range (Practical instruction in remedying Stoppages)	
	8/11/16	8.50 10am	Physical Training NCOs Map reading	
		10.15 12.15	Firing on Range	[initials]
		1.50 3.0pm	Section Drill with arms	
		3.15 4.15	Packing Limbered Wagons	
	9/10/16	9.10 10am	Overhauling guns & Stoppages	
		10.15 11am	Physical Training & Map Reading for NCOs	[initials]
		11.15 12.15	Advanced M.G. Drill	

4353 Wt. W2544/1454 700,000 5/15 D. D. & L. A.D.S.S. Forms/C 2118.

Instructions regarding War Diaries and Intelligence Summaries are contained in F. S. Regs., Part II. and the Staff Manual respectively. Title pages will be prepared in manuscript.

WAR DIARY
or
~~INTELLIGENCE SUMMARY~~. 183 M G Co

(Erase heading not required.)

Army Form C. 2118.

Place	Date	Hour	Summary of Events and Information	Remarks and references to Appendices
In the Field	9/11/16	2 to 4 pm	M.G. Competition Barr & Stroud adjustment.	
	10/11/16	9 to 10 am	Overhauling Guns and Stoppages.	
		10.15 11 am	Physical Training, & N C O's Map Reading	
		11.15 to 12.45 pm	Advanced M.G. Drill & Barr & Stroud Adjustment.	
	11/11/16		Parades for Divine Service as under:—	
			C of E	
		10.15 am	R C	
		~~10.15 am~~	~~[illegible]~~ Section cleaned guns & oiled them & also filled belts.	
	12/11/16	8.50 to 9.45 am	Physical Training & N C O's map reading & Range taking.	
		10.0 to 11.0 am	Fitting & testing Box Respirators	
		11.15 to 12.15	Advanced M.G. Drill combined with concealment.	
		2 to 4 pm	P	
	13/11/16	8.50 10 am	Physical Training & N C O's map reading	
		10.15 to 11 am	Advanced M.G. Drill (wearing Box Respirators)	

2353 Wt. W2544/1454 700,000 5/15 D. D. & L. A.D.S.S. Forms/C. 2118.

Army Form C. 2118.

Instructions regarding War Diaries and Intelligence Summaries are contained in F. S. Regs., Part II. and the Staff Manual respectively. Title pages will be prepared in manuscript.

WAR DIARY
or
~~INTELLIGENCE SUMMARY.~~
(Erase heading not required.)

183 MGCo

Place	Date	Hour	Summary of Events and Information	Remarks and references to Appendices
In the Field	13/11/16	11.15 to 12.15.	Lecture on Indirect & Overhead Fire	
		2 to 4 pm	Firing MGs Rifles + Revolvers on therange.	
	14/11/16	9 am to 10 am	Concealment	
		10.15 am & 11.0 am	Physical Training + NCOs map reading.	
		11.15 to 12.15	Indication + Recognition of Targets.	
		2 pm to 4 pm	Firing Guns + Rifles on range.	
←	15/11/16		The company paraded full marching order, material packed on limbers + marched to Fransu + proceeded to Billets.	
←	16/11/16		Company paraded full marching order, with limbers packed + marched to La Vicogne. + proceeded to make billets as habitable as possible.	
←	17/11/16		Company paraded + marched to Warloy, and took over section of tents allotted to us.	
←	18/11/16		Company paraded + marched to billets situated ~~at~~ in Martinsart.	
←	19/11/16		Advanced Drill with Gas Respirator on + Physical Training	

2353 Wt. W2544/1454 700,000 5/15 D. D. & L. A.D.S.S. Forms/C. 2118.

Instructions regarding War Diaries and Intelligence Summaries are contained in F. S. Regs., Part II. and the Staff Manual respectively. Title pages will be prepared in manuscript.

WAR DIARY
or
~~INTELLIGENCE SUMMARY.~~
(Erase heading not required.)

183 M.G. Coy

Army Form C. 2118.

Place	Date	Hour	Summary of Events and Information	Remarks and references to Appendices
In the Field	20/11/16		Physical Training in Morning with General Overhauling of limbers & greasing of same	[initials]
			Afternoon Bathing Parade	
	21/11/16		Morning Pay parade & Physical Training.	
			Afternoon Overhauling spare parts, limbers packed	
	22/11/16		Company paraded & marched to Billets assigned to this company at Albert. Capt. [illegible] reported missing, Lt. G.G. [illegible] took Command	[initials]
	23/11/16	9.0 am to 9.30	Physical Training	
		9.30 to 10	Instruction re - Chilled Feet etc	
		10 to 11 am	Infantry Drill	[initials]
		11.15 to 12.0	Practice with Box Respirators.	
		2.0 to 4.0	Overhauling Limbers & material.	
	24/11/16	7.30 to 8.0	Physical Training	
		9.0 to 12.0	Advanced Drill & remedying Stoppages with auxiliary mounting & wearing respirators.	[initials]
		2 to 3 pm	Immediate Action	

2353 Wt. W2544/1454 700,000 5/15 D. D. & L. A.D.S.S. Forms/C. 2118.

Instructions regarding War Diaries and Intelligence Summaries are contained in F. S. Regs., Part II. and the Staff Manual respectively. Title pages will be prepared in manuscript.

WAR DIARY
or
~~INTELLIGENCE SUMMARY~~.
(Erase heading not required.)

183 M G Co

Army Form C. 2118.

Place	Date	Hour	Summary of Events and Information	Remarks and references to Appendices
In the Field	24/11/16	3.6 4	Drill (Attached men will continue special instruction on the gun	[initials]
	25/11/16	7.30 8.0 am	Physical Training	
		9.0 to 12	Advanced Drill + consolidation of position including method of constructing open emplacements	[initials]
		2.0 to 3.0	Cleaning + inspection of guns + rifles.	
		3.0 to 4 pm	Instruction in the remedy of stoppages.	
	26/11/16		Company paraded + marched towards Martinsart and occupied Huts assigned to this company at W10 c 3.7 Map France Sheet 57d.	[initials]
	27/11/16	7.30 to 8	Physical Training	
		9 to 12	~~Advanced~~ Construction of open emplacements and addition of overhead cover	[initials]
		2 to 3	Gun Drill	
		3 to 4	Stoppages + repairs.	

2353 Wt. W2544/1454 700,000 5/15 D. D. & L. A.D.S.S. Forms/C 2118.

WAR DIARY
or
~~INTELLIGENCE SUMMARY.~~
(*Erase heading not required.*)

183 M.G. Coy

Army Form C. 2118.

Instructions regarding War Diaries and Intelligence Summaries are contained in F. S. Regs., Part II. and the Staff Manual respectively. Title pages will be prepared in manuscript.

Place	Date	Hour	Summary of Events and Information	Remarks and references to Appendices
In the Field	28/11/16	7.30–8.0	Physical Training	
		9.0–12.0	Improving Emplacements & overhead cover	
		2.0–3.0	Mechanism & Stoppages	
		3.0–4.0	Drill with Respirators. Reconnaissance of Grandcourt – Boom Ravine front.	[illegible]
	29/11/16	7.30–8.0	Physical Training	
		9.0–12.0	Advanced Drill & use of cover. Reconnaissance of Boom Ravine – Grandcourt front.	[illegible]
		2.0–4.0	Overhauling Guns, Belts, Equipment, & packing limbers	
	30/11/16		The company marched from Billets & effected a relief in Grandcourt & Ravine Sector. Maps Grandcourt Edition 4 Ravine Edition 3. Company Headquarters at Mouquet Farm. Relieved company 184 M.G. Coy. Relief completed 2.45 pm. – one casualty. – 12 guns in line.	

2.12.16.

Picking D. Perry Lt.
O.C. 183 M.G. Coy.

Vol 7

CONFIDENTIAL

WAR DIARY.

183 M.G.Coy.

DECEMBER 1916

Instructions regarding War Diaries and Intelligence Summaries are contained in F. S. Regs., Part II. and the Staff Manual respectively. Title pages will be prepared in manuscript.

WAR DIARY
or
~~INTELLIGENCE SUMMARY.~~
(Erase heading not required.)

183 M G Coy

Army Form C. 2118.

Place	Date	Hour	Summary of Events and Information	Remarks and references to Appendices
In the Field	1/12/16		During yesterday this company relieved 184 M G Coy (WM) with 12 guns. The relief completed by 2.45 pm. During the relief of Regina left gun the parties were shelled but sustained no casualties. Boom Ravine was also shelled during relief & 1 casualty was reported. Enemy artillery has searched at irregular intervals Boom Ravine. There was no enemy M G fire here last night.	ERW
	2.12.16		Shelling of both sides of Boom Ravine continued intermittently throughout the day and increasing on the Eastern slopes to a heavy fire at about 1.45pm. No enemy M.G. fire was noticed. Work has been done in improving and repairing quarters. Left Regina front line positions were evacuated at dark by the gun team occupying it.	ERW
	3.12.16		Enemy artillery was active all day on both sides of the Ravine & towards Field Trench both with 5.9s & shrapnel.	E R Warde Lt

Instructions regarding War Diaries and Intelligence Summaries are contained in F. S. Regs., Part II. and the Staff Manual respectively. Title pages will be prepared in manuscript.

WAR DIARY
or
~~INTELLIGENCE SUMMARY~~.
(Erase heading not required.)

Army Form C. 2118.

183 MG Coy

Place	Date	Hour	Summary of Events and Information	Remarks and references to Appendices
In the Field	3.12.16		Enemy MG. fire was considerable, and was noticed during the night from our forward positions in the Ravine (R22b 9.9) Map. Sheet 57d SE France	
		4.45pm 6.0pm	2000 rds were fired indirectly on area R15b 3.0 – R15b 8.1 – R15b 0.9 – R15b 7 9½ tracks & dugouts.	
			Enemy artillery searched the western ridge of the Ravine briskly	
			The gun withdrawn from the left of Regina line was given a position in Zollern trench R28b 6.8 during the day.	[illegible]
	4.12.16		The Ravine was again shelled during the day especially on the Regina line.	
			Our forward positions came under considerable shell fire during the night, & MG. fire was noticed up the Ravine	
			Work has been done on dugouts of which had to be thoroughly cleaned up, and entrances cleared.	[illegible]

Instructions regarding War Diaries and Intelligence Summaries are contained in F. S. Regs., Part II. and the Staff Manual respectively. Title pages will be prepared in manuscript.

WAR DIARY
or
~~INTELLIGENCE SUMMARY.~~
(Erase heading not required.)

183 M G Coy

Army Form C. 2118.

Place	Date	Hour	Summary of Events and Information	Remarks and references to Appendices
In the Field.	5.12.16		Enemy artillery showed the usual activity but eased down a little after midnight. Open emplacements are being constructed. Indirect Fire was carried out against Grandcourt (R9) & drew artillery retaliation. In all 4,000 rds were fired at intervals from dusk to midnight.	EEW
	6.12.16		Heavy enemy shelling is reported from R22 b 8½ 9½ but no damage from R22 c 2.6. Enemy artillery reported below normal very quiet night. Severe shelling of Coy Hqrs 2.0 – ~~4~~ 4.0 pm. Usual activity with HE & shrapnel in Ravine Ridge. R22 b 8½ 9½ severely ~~[illegible]~~ shelled since 6.0 pm. No Indirect Fire was carried out owing to Infantry relief	EEW
	7.12.16		Enemy activity considerable the day including another bombardment of Coy Hqrs. Reports from gun positions show unusual quiet of enemy ~~side~~.	EEWard

2353 Wt. W2544/1454 700,000 5/15 D. D. & L. A.D.S.S. Forms/C 2118.

Instructions regarding War Diaries and Intelligence Summaries are contained in F. S. Regs., Part II. and the Staff Manual respectively. Title pages will be prepared in manuscript.

WAR DIARY

or

~~INTELLIGENCE SUMMARY~~.

(Erase heading not required.)

183 M G Coy

Army Form C. 2118.

Place	Date	Hour	Summary of Events and Information	Remarks and references to Appendices
In the Field	7.12.16		Light shells were sent over during Indirect fire operation From dusk till midnight indirect fire was carried out against enemy front line on the left (R16b) ravine & roads in R10a & b Only the above retaliation	ERW
	8.12.16		Enemy artillery activity a little below normal. Work on salvage, cleaning up, and work on emplacements has been continued. There is nothing unusual to report	ERW
	9.12.16		Enemy artillery activity was chiefly noticed on the ridge to the left of Ravine. On the whole their artillery was less active than usual	ERW
	[illegible]		Work has been done in Regina trench in providing shelters for a team about R22 a 9.7 Salvage of stores has also been effected. Positions at R.20 d 9.9. & R.21 c. 2.0. were taken over from 34 M G Coy Relief being completed by about 7. pm	E R Ward Lt.

2353 Wt. W2544/1454 700,000 5/15 D. D. & L. A.D.S.S. Forms/C. 2118.

Instructions regarding War Diaries and Intelligence Summaries are contained in F. S. Regs., Part II. and the Staff Manual respectively. Title pages will be prepared in manuscript.

WAR DIARY
or
~~INTELLIGENCE SUMMARY~~.
(Erase heading not required.)

Army Form C. 2118.

183 MG Coy

Place	Date	Hour	Summary of Events and Information	Remarks and references to Appendices
In the Field	10.12.16		Indirect fire was carried out from dusk till midnight on the left positions of Grandcourt. Enemy artillery activity on usual points about the Ravine and shrapnel over duckboards tracks etc, leading to Tullochs Corner; intermittent shelling by 5.9s about Tullochs Corner. This company was relieved during the evening at 5.30 pm - 6.0 pm by 182 MG Coy + moved to Huts near Martinsart ~~and~~ Company Hqrs situated in Martinsart.	ERW
	11.12.16		The day was spent in cleaning clothes, equipment, and collecting stores etc; + packing limbers.	ERW
	12.12.16		Company paraded and marched to Billets at Hedauville + the rest of the day was spent in cleaning huts unloading stores etc.	ERW
	13.12.16		Physical Training and fatigues on clearing mud from tracks, digging trenches for draining purposes, laying duckboards + supply Town Major with guard for water troughs.	E.R.W[illegible]

2353 Wt. W2544/1454 700,000 5/15 D. D. & L. A.D.S.S. Forms/C. 2118.

Army Form C. 2118.

WAR DIARY
or
~~INTELLIGENCE SUMMARY~~.
(Erase heading not required.)

183 M G Coy

Instructions regarding War Diaries and Intelligence Summaries are contained in F. S. Regs., Part II. and the Staff Manual respectively. Title pages will be prepared in manuscript.

Place	Date	Hour	Summary of Events and Information	Remarks and references to Appendices
In the Field	14.12.16	9.0am to 12.30	Overhauling & cleaning of all kit & equipment, & reports taken of all deficiencies	
		2.15 to 3.15	Stoppages and Mechanism	ERW
	15.12.16	9–9.30 am	Physical Training, N.C.O's Lecture Indirect Fire (1)	
		9.30 to 10.0 am	Gun Drill.	
		10.30 to 11.15	Stoppages and Mechanism	
		11.30 to 12.30	Advanced Drill with Respirators.	
		2.15 to 3.15	Firing with Respirators on	ERW
	16.12.16	9.0 to 12.30	Making open emplacements with addition of overhead cover	
		2.15 to 3.15pm	Football	ERW
	17.12.16		Church Parade.	ERW
	18.12.16	9.0 to 9.30am	Physical Training N.C.O's Lecture Indirect Fire (2)	
		9.30am to 10.0	Gun Drill	
		10.15 to 12.30	Route March	
		2.15 to 3.15pm	Advanced Drill	ERW
	19.12.16	9.0 to 9.30am	Physical Training	

E.R. Ward Lt

2353 Wt. W2544/1454 700,000 5/15 D. D. & L. A.D.S.S. Forms/C. 2118.

Instructions regarding War Diaries and Intelligence Summaries are contained in F. S. Regs., Part II. and the Staff Manual respectively. Title pages will be prepared in manuscript.

WAR DIARY
or
~~INTELLIGENCE SUMMARY.~~
(Erase heading not required.)

183 M G Coy

Army Form C. 2118.

Place	Date	Hour	Summary of Events and Information	Remarks and references to Appendices
In the Field	19.12.16	9.45am to 12.30	Range Work.	
		2.15 to 3.15pm	Firing.	[illegible]
	20.12.16	9.0 to 12.30	Advanced Drill.	
		2.45pm to 9.45	Physical Training.	
		2.45 to 3.15pm	Drill.	[illegible]
	21.12.16	9.0 to 9.30am	Physical Training	
		9.30 to 10.30am	Gun Drill.	
		10.30 to 12.30am	Cleaning & Packing Limbers	
		2.15 to 3.45pm	Football.	[illegible]
	22.12.16		Company paraded and marched to Huts by Martinsart Wood & the Rest of the day was spent unloading stores & settling in billets, cleaning away mud etc.	
	23.12.16		Rifle, revolver and equipment inspection during the morning	[illegible]
		4.30 to 11.30pm	Men marched to X 22.a.3.2. for working party under R.Es working in Trenches.	
	24.12.16		Fatigue working party as above & Church Parade.	[illegible]

[illegible]

Instructions regarding War Diaries and Intelligence Summaries are contained in F. S. Regs., Part II. and the Staff Manual respectively. Title pages will be prepared in manuscript.

WAR DIARY
or
~~INTELLIGENCE SUMMARY.~~
(Erase heading not required.)

183 M G Coy

Army Form C. 2118.

Place	Date	Hour	Summary of Events and Information	Remarks and references to Appendices
In the Field	25/12/16	8.0 to 11.30 am	Fatigue work on roads draining etc as per table received from Bde	
	26/12/16	7.0 to 2 pm	Fatigue working parties as per Brigade table received.	[illegible]
		7.0 to 2 pm	Fatigue working party in trenches as per table	[illegible]
	28/12/16	~~7.0 to~~ 5 pm	This company paraded & marched to Mouquet Farm & relieved 184 M G Coy in the line. Relief completed by 5 pm	[illegible]
	29/12/16		During the last 24 hours enemy artillery has been fairly active. Hessian & Field Trenches were shelled at intervals with H.E. & shrapnel throughout the day.	[illegible]
	30/12/16		Yesterday from 9.0 am till about 2.45 pm enemy artillery activity was considerable on Hessian & Regina trenches. Our artillery effectively dealt with them. Situation yesterday & last night normal. Work in connection with the cleaning out of emplacements, dugouts, and getting rid of the water etc was performed.	E Edwards Lt

2353 Wt. W2544/1454 700,000 5/15 D. D. & L. A.D.S.S. Forms/C 2118.

Instructions regarding War Diaries and Intelligence Summaries are contained in F. S. Regs., Part II. and the Staff Manual respectively. Title pages will be prepared in manuscript.

WAR DIARY

or

~~INTELLIGENCE SUMMARY~~.

(Erase heading not required.)

183 M G Coy

Army Form C. 2118.

Place	Date	Hour	Summary of Events and Information	Remarks and references to Appendices
In the Field	31.12.16		Enemy artillery activity was very considerable. Regina Trench & the Ravine was heavily shelled in the afternoon & Hessian received treatment with HE. at intervals during the day. Indirect fire was carried out on R 9 a 9.7. during the night. No retaliation. Work was done of a general tidying nature and an extra emplacement has been built during the night.	E Edwards Lt for O.C. 183 M.G. Coy

2353 Wt. W2544/1454 700,000 5/15 D. D. & L. A.D.S.S. Forms/C. 2118.

Vol 8

War Diary

— of —

183rd Machine Gun Company

— for —

January 1917

Instructions regarding War Diaries and Intelligence Summaries are contained in F. S. Regs., Part II. and the Staff Manual respectively. Title pages will be prepared in manuscript.

WAR DIARY
or
~~INTELLIGENCE SUMMARY.~~
(*Erase heading not required.*)

183 MG Coy

Army Form C. 2118.

Place	Date	Hour	Summary of Events and Information	Remarks and references to Appendices
In the Field	1/1/17		Enemy artillery was rather considerable: Regina Trench and the Ravine were steadily but heavily shelled during the afternoon, Hessian trench especially to the left received a considerable number of HE's at intervals throughout the day. Indirect Fire was carried out on R9a97 during the night at intervals. There was no retaliation. Work of a general clean up and tidying nature was performed dugouts & emplacements thoroughly cleaned out etc, and an extra emplacement has been started upon	
	2.1.17		During the morning of yesterday, hostile artillery lightly shelled our positions near Hessian, increasing during the afternoon and seemed directed towards Field Trench as well. Between 9.0 & 10.30 pm there was a particularly heavy artillery dual. Since then the situation has been normal Work in connection with building emplacements facilitating more rapid ~~construction~~ mounting of the gun, and also in connection with Defence Scheme has been done Special Situation Report. From 12.45pm – 2.15pm Mouquet Farm was heavily shelled with 4.2's, 5.9s 8inch and shrapnel. About 150 shelled were fired. No casualties in this unit.	

A5834 Wt. W4973/M687 750,000 8/16 D. D. & L. Ltd. Forms/C.2118/13.

Instructions regarding War Diaries and Intelligence Summaries are contained in F. S. Regs., Part II. and the Staff Manual respectively. Title pages will be prepared in manuscript.

WAR DIARY
or
~~INTELLIGENCE SUMMARY.~~
(Erase heading not required.)

183 M.G. Coy

Army Form C. 2118.

Place	Date	Hour	Summary of Events and Information	Remarks and references to Appendices
In the Field	3/1/17		Yesterday hostile artillery was above normal. Hessian and Field trenches were shelled with H.E. and Shrapnel at intervals while at 2pm the enemy searched between Zollern Redoubt and Mouquet Farm and shelled the latter heavily. 2nd Assembly trench and Rifle Dump received a rather severe amount of shelling: this was replied to by our artillery actively.	
			During the night we engaged targets with our Indirect Fire at R10 b 2½ 2 and swept the reverse slopes in R10 c & d (Map sheet 57d SE	
			Work is still progressing ~~at~~ on Open emplacements	
	4.1.17		Hostile artillery activity was below normal, light shelling is taking place at intervals in the direction of Hessian Trench. Our own artillery was fairly active.	
			Work was done on repairing dugouts, and making open emplacements	
			Between 8 & 9 pm about 100 gas shells were dropped in the vicinity of Mouquet Farm. Owing to the strong wind the effect was nil	

A5834 Wt. W4973/M687 750,000 8/16 D. D. & L. Ltd. Forms/C.2118/13.

Instructions regarding War Diaries and Intelligence Summaries are contained in F. S. Regs., Part II. and the Staff Manual respectively. Title pages will be prepared in manuscript.

WAR DIARY
or
~~INTELLIGENCE~~ SUMMARY.
(Erase heading not required.)

183 M G Coy

Army Form C. 2118.

Place	Date	Hour	Summary of Events and Information	Remarks and references to Appendices
In the Field.	5/1/17		During the past 24 hours Hessian left was shelled fairly heavily with HE and Shrapnel. Our artillery were active all the afternoon & shelled enemy lines. Practically no retaliation. Several of our aeroplanes were up during the afternoon the atmosphere being perfectly clear. At 6·20pm an unknown aeroplane passed over R21d & went to the left. There was a slight bombardment by the enemy at 11.15 pm – our artillery retaliated strongly, and shelling continued on both sides between 1am & 3am. During the night we swept obscure ground in R10 a rd with indirect M.G. fire at intervals	
	6.1.17		Yesterday Hessian & Field Trenches were as usual heavily bombarded with HE and Shrapnel. Towards evening our artillery became very active. On the left of our front there seemed to be a heavy bombardment from 11 pm to 1am. The enemy put up red lights at 6pm. Work on emplacements continued.	

A5834 Wt. W4973/M687 750,000 8/16 D. D. & L. Ltd. Forms/C.2118/13.

Instructions regarding War Diaries and Intelligence Summaries are contained in F. S. Regs., Part II. and the Staff Manual respectively. Title pages will be prepared in manuscript.

WAR DIARY
or
~~INTELLIGENCE SUMMARY.~~
(Erase heading not required.)

183 M G Coy

Army Form C. 2118.

Place	Date	Hour	Summary of Events and Information	Remarks and references to Appendices
In the Field	6.1.17		This company was relieved in the line by 182 M G Coy the company marched upon relief to Huts situated near Martinsart. Hqrs at Martinsart.	
	7/1/17		This day was spent in seeing to gun equipment re-packing of limbers, cleaning clothes etc.	
	8/1/17		The company paraded and marched to Hedauville and took up billets in huts. P34 c 3.7.	
	9/1/17		Day was spent in unloading stores, seeing to equipment cleaning same, and rifles & revolvers, and working on drainage, paths etc, & general cleaning up of place.	
	10/1/17	9.0-9.30	Physical Training	
		9.30-11.30	Inspection of Kit, Clothing, Boots Iron Rations etc.	
		11.45-12.45	Cleaning Guns	
		2.0-3.0	Checking Spare Parts	
	11/1/17	9.0-9.30	Physical Training	
		9.30-10.30	Stoppages	
		11.0-12.30	Washing Limbers	
		2.0-3.0	Filling Belts for Firing	

A5834 Wt. W4973/M687 750,000 8/16 D. D. & L. Ltd. Forms/C.2118/13.

Instructions regarding War Diaries and Intelligence Summaries are contained in F. S. Regs., Part II. and the Staff Manual respectively. Title pages will be prepared in manuscript.

WAR DIARY
or
~~INTELLIGENCE SUMMARY.~~
(*Erase heading not required.*)

183 M G Coy

Army Form C. 2118.

Place	Date	Hour	Summary of Events and Information	Remarks and references to Appendices
In the Field	12/1/17	9 - 9.30	Physical Training	
		~~9.35-12.15~~ 9.30-10.30	Stoppages	
		10.45-12.15	March Discipline	
		2.0 - 3.0 pm	Cleaning Guns	
	13/1/17	9.0-9.30	Physical Training	
		9.45-10.45	Mechanism	
		10.45-12.15	March Discipline	
		2.0-3.0 pm	Cleaning Guns, Belt Boxes etc	
HEDEAUVILLE	14-1-17		Church Parades.	
"	15-1-17		Cleaning and greasing limbers preparatory to moving. Packing stores etc.	
BEAUQUESNE	16-1-17		Company marched with 183 Infantry Bde to Billets at BEAUQUESNE arriving in billets at 2.30 PM, having started at 9.25 AM. Route via VARENNES – LEALVILLERS – ARQUEVES – RAINCHEVAL.	
GRIMONT.	17-1-17		Company marched in conjunct with 183 Inf: Bde to GRIMONT starting at 8.40 AM, reaching Billets at 4 PM. Route via Fm de ROSEL – CANDAS – FIENVILLERS – BERNAVILLE – PROUVILLE.	
CONTEVILLE	18-1-17		Company marched in conjunction with 183 Inf. Bde to CONTEVILLE starting 10.0 AM, reaching Billets 12 noon. Route via PROUVILLE – AGENVILLE.	
ARGENVILLERS	19-1-17		Coy marched to ARGENVILLERS in conjunction with 183 Inf: Bde, start 10.40 AM reaching billets at	

A5834 Wt. W4973/M687 750,000 8/16 D. D. & L. Ltd. Forms/C.2118/13.

Army Form C. 2118.

Instructions regarding War Diaries and Intelligence Summaries are contained in F. S. Regs., Part II. and the Staff Manual respectively. Title pages will be prepared in manuscript.

WAR DIARY
or
~~INTELLIGENCE SUMMARY.~~
(Erase heading not required.)

Place	Date	Hour	Summary of Events and Information	Remarks and references to Appendices
ARGENVILLERS	19-1-17		3PM. Route via YVRENCH – CAPENNES. This is the destination of the Coy.	
"	20-1-17		General cleaning up and resting.	
"	21-1-17		Church Parades.	
"	22-1-17		Cleaning and washing Limbers. Cleaning Guns and tidying up Gun stores	
"	23-1-17		General training } The Company were trained in the following:–	
"	24-1-17		General training } Description of parts of Gun. Care and cleaning	
"	25-1-17		General Training } Stripping. Points before, during, and after firing	Training area ref
"	26-1-17		General training } Action of Mechanism	
"	27-1-17		General Training } Immediate Action	
"	28-1-17		Church parades 10AM 3.30PM.	ST. RIQUIER 1/20000
"	29-1-17		General training } Including the following:–	A.16.b.
"	30-1-17		General Training } Map Reading. Immediate action	
"	31-1-17		General training } Indication and Recognition of Targets. Tr. on gun range	

S.H. Leck Mt.
OC
183 M G Coy

A5834 Wt. W4973/M687 750,000 8/16 D. D. & L. Ltd. Forms/C.2118/13.

February 1917

Vol 9

War Diary

of

183 Machine Gun Company.

Army Form C. 2118.

WAR DIARY
or
~~INTELLIGENCE SUMMARY.~~
(Erase heading not required.)

183 M.G. Coy.

Instructions regarding War Diaries and Intelligence Summaries are contained in F. S. Regs., Part II. and the Staff Manual respectively. Title pages will be prepared in manuscript.

Place.	Date	Hour	Summary of Events and Information	Remarks and references to Appendices
ARGENVILLERS	1-2-17		General Training, range practice during the morning. The Corps Commander visited M.G. Coy during range practice. Inspection of Transport by Brigadier, who expressed satisfaction.	
"	2-2-17		General Training in the morning. First round of Football competition played in the afternoon M.G. Coy beat 2/2 Field Ambulance.	General Training filling belts
"	3-2-17 4-2-17		Cleaning and greasing limbers preparatory to move. Church Parades	
"	5-2-17		183 M.G. Coy together with 182 & 184 M.G. Coys marched to LE CROTOY (mouth of SOMME) Billeted at ST FIRMIN (4 miles from LE CROTOY). Started 9AM destination reached at 3.30PM. No men fell out, marching good. Transport had 3 pairs of Lead Mules taken away and attached to A.S.C. Train.	
ST. FIRMIN.	6-2-17		Range work on seashore, ranging and application 400 yds. Rows 9AM – 2PM	
"	7-2-17		Range work 9AM – 5PM. ranging & application 400 yds & 500 yds, Service application 500 yds.	
"	8-2-17		9AM – 2PM range work Service application 500 yds	
"	9-2-17		Demonstrations of Barrage fire at 1500 yds & 1800 yds. Combined sights. Experiments with 'Sparklet Ammunition' or Tracer bullets. Found satisfactory up to 700 yds not over. All demonstrations under Corps M.G. Officer	
"	10-2-17		182, 183, & 184 M.G. Coy marched to HAUTVILLERS starting 9AM arriving BILLETS at 3 P.M. HAUTVILLERS 7½ Kilom: from ABBEVILLE.	
"	11-2-17		183 M.G. Coy rejoined 183 Infantry Brigade at ERGNIES near AILLY-LE-HAUT CLOCHER. Limbers repacked preparatory to further move.	

A5834 Wt. W4973/M687 750,000 8/16 D. D. & L. Ltd. Forms/C.2118/13.

Instructions regarding War Diaries and Intelligence Summaries are contained in F. S. Regs., Part II. and the Staff Manual respectively. Title pages will be prepared in manuscript.

WAR DIARY
or
~~INTELLIGENCE SUMMARY.~~
(Erase heading not required.)

Army Form C. 2118.

Place	Date	Hour	Summary of Events and Information	Remarks and references to Appendices
~~12-2-17~~ ERGNIES	12-2-17		Company resting. Transport in conjunction with 183 Inf: Bde Transport marched to ST SAUVOUR. Lead Mules returned.	
"	13-2-17		Cleaning up personal attire still resting.	
"	14-2-17		Company marched from ERGNIES at 2AM to PONT REMY arriving 5AM. Company entrained and taken to WIENCOURT (W 7B ref: ROSIÈRES combined sheet 1/40000) Transport rejoin. In billets by 2PM.	
"	15-2-17		Company prepare for Trenches C.O visits trenches around VERMANDOVILLERS (S 9 D central ref map ROSIÈRES)	
FRAMERVILLE	16-2-17		183 M G Coy move in conjunct with 183 Inf: Bde to FRAMERVILLE	
Trenches	17-2-17		At 2AM Company marched to VERMANDOVILLERS and take over M.G. position from French. 6 guns around ABLAINCOURT, 5 around BOIS KRATZ, 5 guns around BOIS AMBERG. relief complete by 8AM. One French M.G.O staying in with each section (Coy divided into 3 as above) H.Q at VERMANDOVILLERS (S15 b 3.0. MAP. VERMANDOVILLER 62c S.W.3 1/10,000). Quiet part of the line generally.	
"	18-2-17		Quiet situation normal. Thaw set in making trenches very muddy. arranging to replace M.G.s in KRATZ WOOD with Lewis Rifles. Withdrawing guns to BOYAU AMBERG second line a line of resistance. Casualties nil. No indirect fire being done by order of Bde.	

A5834 Wt W4973/M687 750,000 8/16 D. D. & L. Ltd. Forms/C.2118/13.

Instructions regarding War Diaries and Intelligence Summaries are contained in F. S. Regs., Part II. and the Staff Manual respectively. Title pages will be prepared in manuscript.

WAR DIARY

or

~~INTELLIGENCE SUMMARY.~~

(Erase heading not required.)

Army Form C. 2118.

Place	Date	Hour	Summary of Events and Information	Remarks and references to Appendices
Trenches	19-2-17		Situation Normal. Thaw making trenches very muddy. All guns in KRATZ wood were withdrawn to positions i BOYAU AMBERG. One gun being withdrawn to H.Q. VERMANDOVILLERS. Two guns were withdrawn from right front line and brought to Coy. H.Q. Artillery activity was slight, a few shells falling in KRATZ Wood. Gas was reported on left in the ROUSKI Sector, men wore gas helmet for a few minutes. Presumedly gas shells. Work done – ammunition carrying & trench stores. French Officers remaining with sections in the line have departed.	
"	20-2-17		Day misty mud increasing making trench work difficult. Trenches slipping in in places as trenches are not reveted. Situation normal artillery quiet. Work done:- improving gun positions. About 6 PM a man approached the gun positions in By AMBERG	
"	21-2-17		coming over the direction. He was challenged but took no notice. He was fired upon but got away.	
"	21-2-17		Situation Normal. Communication bad owing to muddy condition of Trenches. Some points impassable. 6 Gloucesters relieved 4th Gloucesters in left Sub sector (PRESSOIRE) during the night. A battalion of the LANCS FUSILIERS relieved French on our extreme right. Enemy aerial torpedoes active near left MG positions L S. 24.a (Map VERMANDOVILLERS 1/10000). Our Artillery registered Enemy trenches throughout the day. KRATZ wood shelled intermittently throughout the day. Coy. H.Q. at LEAUTEY was shelled about 11 PM with 4.2. Enemy M Gs quiet. Snipers quiet.	

A5834 Wt. W4973/M687 750,000 8/16 D. D. & L. Ltd. Forms/C.2118/13.

Instructions regarding War Diaries and Intelligence Summaries are contained in F. S. Regs., Part II. and the Staff Manual respectively. Title pages will be prepared in manuscript.

WAR DIARY
or
~~INTELLIGENCE SUMMARY.~~

(Erase heading not required.)

Army Form C. 2118.

Place	Date	Hour	Summary of Events and Information	Remarks and references to Appendices
Trenches KRATZ SOUS-SECTOR	22-2-17		Artillery on both sides quiet. Mud upsetting communications but owing to a thick mist it has been possible to walk over the top. Several enemy aerial torpedoes fell near our M.G. Emplacement around ABLAINCOURT. There has been sniping in RIGHT SECTOR. Work preventing the mud entering dug-outs, strengthening M.G. Emplacements. Situat. normal.	
"	23-2-17		Situat. normal. Mist prevented observation and communicat. was again possible over the top. Trenches still very muddy being impassable in places. At 7.50 PM Enemy opened an intense bombardment upon the whole Brigade front. Shelling was mainly concentrated on CHAULNES WOOD just in rear of our front line from S.29.a.1.9. to Battalion on our right flank, on X rds. S22, &37 and N end of KRATZ WOOD. One of our M.G. in front line fired upon a German M.G. an occasional burst was fired into No mans land. Right gun of Centre Sector was knocked over by explosion of a shell but no damage done.	
"	24-2-17		~~Situat.~~ Situation normal. Enemy Artillery showed more activity during early afternoon around KRATZ WOOD. BOYAU AMBERG was shelled with Shrapnel. A dummy raid was carried out by us at 8 PM lasting for 8 minutes. Six M.G.s fired on following targets 2 guns S30.c.0.6 – S30.c.4.6. 3 guns S30.c.1.6. – S29.d.6.3. 1 gun S.30.A.7.1. – S30.G.9.9. firing 3,500 rounds. Work clearing mud away from vicinity of Emplacements.	
"	25-2-17		At 4 AM 182 M.G. Coy arrived at VERMANDOVILLERS to relieve 183 M.G. Coy. relief completed by 10.15 AM. a dense mist made relief easy as all gun teams could move over top. 183 M.G. Coy marched to HARBONNIERES arriving in billets at about 4 PM. One officer per section & one man per gun team spent day with 182 M.G. Coy coming out at dusk. 3 men reported sick during this tour of trenches.	

A5834 Wt. W4973/M687 750,000 8/16 D. D. & L. Ltd. Forms/C.2118/13.

Instructions regarding War Diaries and Intelligence Summaries are contained in F. S. Regs., Part II. and the Staff Manual respectively. Title pages will be prepared in manuscript.

WAR DIARY
or
~~INTELLIGENCE SUMMARY.~~
(Erase heading not required.)

Army Form C. 2118.

Place	Date	Hour	Summary of Events and Information	Remarks and references to Appendices
HARBONNIERES	26-2-17		In rest Billets. Day spent in cleaning clothing guns etc. At 6 PM No 1 & 2 Sections billet caught fire. The billet, which contained large quantities of straw was completely gutted. Several out houses were also burnt. The fire was localized by about 8 PM. 3 guns were rendered useless 44 mens blankets equipment etc destroyed. The Company worked in reliefs through out the night 26/27 intil until daylight. Great assistance & consideration was shown us by Col. DORMAN who placed his battalion 2/7 WORCESTERS at our disposal.	
"	27-2-17		Fire still smouldering in billets, a picquet of six men being kept on guard over material etc. Gun cleaning. Kit inspections all day. Lists of government property lost in fire made out estimated damage value of £ 1358-8-9. Estimated damage done to civilian property not yet fixed. All fighting limbers brought from FRAMERVILLE to HARBONNIERES.	
"	28-2-17		Baths ~~8~~ 9 AM & 7 PM - 8 PM. for 80 men. No clean clothing available. General training 9 AM - 12 noon & 2 PM - 3 PM.	

[illegible] Field
28-2-17

S. h Leck Capt
O.C
183 M G Coy

A5834 Wt. W4973/M687 750,000 8/16 D. D. & L. Ltd. Forms/C.2118/13.

March 1917

Vol ~~8~~ 10

War Diary

– of –

183 Machine Gun Coy

Instructions regarding War Diaries and Intelligence Summaries are contained in F. S. Regs., Part II. and the Staff Manual respectively. Title pages will be prepared in manuscript.

WAR DIARY
or
~~INTELLIGENCE SUMMARY.~~ 183 M.G. Coy

(Erase heading not required.)

Army Form C. 2118.

Place	Date	Hour	Summary of Events and Information	Remarks and references to Appendices
HARBONNIERES	1-3-17		General Training. Fire still smouldering } Physical drill, Stoppages, Mechanism, Gun drill	
"	2-3-17		General Training. Baths.	
"	3-3-17		General training. Lecture for Officers on Artillery & Infantry Co-operation. Fire completely out.	
"	4-3-17		General training, range work. Lecture by Corps M.G. Officer.	
"	5-3-17		General training } Mechanism, stoppages, Gun drill, range, Methods of Indirect fire.	
"	6-3-17		General training }	
"	7-3-17		preparations for trenches.	
Trenches	8-3-17		183 M.G. Coy relieved 182 M.G. Coy in the SOUS KRATZ Sector (6 guns). Enemy very quiet, the relief completed by 10 P.M. without a hitch. Weather conditions good. Coy H.Q. in VERMANDOVILLERS. Left boundary of Bde road running through A PRESSOIRE.	
"	9-3-17		Situation normal. Very clear day up to 3 P.M., then snow. We relieved 3 guns of 106 M.G. Coy in BOIS TRIANGULAIRE. Right Bde boundary now road LIHONS – CHAULNES. 183 M.G. Coy now has 9 guns in the line, 3 guns at VERMANDOVILLERS and 4 guns in billets at FRAMERVILLE, 5 kilos behind line. Enemy artillery exceptionally quiet. A few 5.9 on right of BOIS TRIANGULAIRE.	
"	10-3-17		Situation normal. A few aerial torpedoes fell in KRATZ wood during the morning. G.O.C. Division visited right Sector, approves of M.G. dispositions.	
"	11-3-17		Artillery activity slightly below normal, except hostile AA guns which were kept busy all day firing at our aeroplanes. There was also considerable M/C gun fire against our aircraft.	

A5834 Wt. W4973/M687 750,000 8/16 D. D. & L. Ltd. Forms/C.2118/13.

Instructions regarding War Diaries and Intelligence Summaries are contained in F. S. Regs., Part II. and the Staff Manual respectively. Title pages will be prepared in manuscript.

WAR DIARY
or
~~INTELLIGENCE SUMMARY.~~
(Erase heading not required.)

Army Form C. 2118.

Place	Date	Hour	Summary of Events and Information	Remarks and references to Appendices
Trenches	11.3.17		We applied Indirect fire against left edge of Chaulnes during the evening. Work was done cleaning + finishing our open emplacement.	
	12.3.17		Enemy artillery quiet for last 24 hours. H.E fell forward of S.C Chaulnes + AMBERG TRENCH was slightly shelled in the afternoon. Enemy m.g's fired in bursts between 6.30 7.30pm + 9.0 to 10.pm against our front line. Indirect fire from positions A5a 3.7 + S23c 5.7 was applied to Chaulnes between 8.0pm + 12 midnight. Fire from the latter position was stopped at 8.15pm. Targets (1) A5b0.4 (2) A5d9.3. A new m.g. emplacement was built at A3b 7.7. Coy Hqrs moved to just off Serpentin Tr.	
	13.3.17		Hostile artillery slightly more active than usual. Kratz Wood shelled in the evening. Enemy M.G. fired as though sniping. Indirect fire was carried out by guns as follows. No 1 gun position at A5c½ 5 over area A5a 4.0, A11.a½ 7 A5d½ 9 A11a 5.4 from 12 am to 1am. 2 gun position fired at ... from 10.30am to 5.0am	
	14.3.17		Enemy artillery slightly above normal. Polygon Wood in region of front line and LIHONS was shelled with heavy calibre shells between 1.0 – 1.30pm. During the day Indirect fire was applied to CHAULNES A11a + A5d.	
	15.3.17		Enemy artillery activity below normal increasing for a time at 3pm while one of his aeroplanes was up. Our m/g's carried out indirect fire during the day and night sweeping at intervals ground in A5c, 4d, + 11a. + enemy communications in B1a–1b. Internal relief completed by 8.0pm	

A5834 Wt. W4973/M687 750,000 8/16 D. D. & L. Ltd. Forms/C.2118/13.

Army Form C. 2118.

WAR DIARY
or
~~INTELLIGENCE SUMMARY.~~
(Erase heading not required.)

Instructions regarding War Diaries and Intelligence Summaries are contained in F. S. Regs., Part II. and the Staff Manual respectively. Title pages will be prepared in manuscript.

Place	Date	Hour	Summary of Events and Information	Remarks and references to Appendices
Trenches	16.3.17		Enemy artillery activity normal. M.Gs + snipers active chiefly against aeroplanes. From 6.0pm to 9.0pm enemy m.g fired at some target behind left section Hqrs. Enemy artillery ~~activity~~ retaliation was weak. Our guns carried out Indirect fire against A5a & c at irregular intervals during the day.	
	17.3.17		Slight artillery action during the morning, and none during the afternoon. Strong patrols sent out found enemy trenches in region of Chaulnes evacuated and pushed forward as far as Railway at Omiecourt.	
	18.3.17		During the morning Company Hqrs moved from Vermandovillers to P.C. Amberg. 2 Sections took up quarters in Chaulnes, 1 section moved forward with Infantry to Omiecourt. Patrols passed through Pertain, Dreslincourt etc.	
	19.3.17		Coy Hqrs moved forward via Chaulnes, Omiecourt to Dreslincourt. 1 Section moved to Hyencourt, 1 to Dreslincourt, & 1 to Potte.	
	20.3.17		8 guns moved up and held line from Morchain to Mesnil-St Nicaise.	
	21.3.17		Left flank 4 guns moved from Morchain to Bethencourt.	
	22.3.17		Dispositions remained the same.	
	23.3.17		Dispositions remained the same	

A5834 Wt. W4973/M687 750,000 8/16 D. D. & L. Ltd. Forms/C.2118/13.

Instructions regarding War Diaries and Intelligence Summaries are contained in F. S. Regs., Part II. and the Staff Manual respectively. Title pages will be prepared in manuscript.

WAR DIARY
or
~~INTELLIGENCE SUMMARY.~~
(Erase heading not required.)

Army Form C. 2118.

Place	Date	Hour	Summary of Events and Information	Remarks and references to Appendices
In the field	24.3.17		The day and night ~~were~~ passed without particular interest. Shelling was heard at intervals some distance off. Under instructions from Brigade 2 guns have been moved forward from reserve to CROIX-MOLYNEUX. + 2 guns have been sent back to Potte.	
	25.3.17		Day and night quiet. Coy Hqrs + 4 guns moved forward from DRESLINCOURT to MORCHAIN. + 4 guns from Mesnil-St Nicaise to Morchain.	
	26.3.17		Day and night passed quietly. Guns at CROIX-MOLYNEUX were placed as follows:- D5a 2.4, D9a 8.2, D9a 2.8, D8b 3.9½ covering approaches to the village.	
	27.3.17		Transport and Stores moved up to MORCHAIN during the morning. Position in the line CAULINCOURT – TREFCON reconnoitred.	
	28.3.17		4 guns in position in Q35c, W5a + c central – 4 guns in position at VILLÉVÊQUE – 4 guns in position forward of TREFCON. Coy Hqrs moved from MORCHAIN via BETHENCOURT picking up 4 guns at the latter place through CROIX-MOLYNEUX to MONCHY-LEGARCHE	
	29.3.17		COULAINCOURT and ETREILLERS were shelled during the day. Gun positions ~~[illegible]~~ established at W11a 9.7 – W11c 3.9½ – W10d 4½.4½ W16d 6 1½. Q35c 4½.0. – W5a 7½.5 – W5c 7½.8½ W5c 9.6	

A5834 Wt W4973/M687 750,000 8/16 D. D. & L. Ltd. Forms/C.2118/13.

Army Form C. 2118.

Instructions regarding War Diaries and Intelligence Summaries are contained in F. S. Regs., Part II. and the Staff Manual respectively. Title pages will be prepared in manuscript.

WAR DIARY
or
~~INTELLIGENCE SUMMARY.~~
(Erase heading not required.)

Place	Date	Hour	Summary of Events and Information	Remarks and references to Appendices
In the field	30·3·17		Day and night were fairly quiet except for some shelling of CAULAINCOURT & VILLEVÊQUE and some activity of our own artillery. The 4 guns at CAULAINCOURT relieved the 4 at TREFCON taking over same positions. The 4 at TREFCON moved forward to VILLEVÊQUE where 2 are in mobile reserve and 2 were posted up to LEAF WOOD in support of infantry there. Positions about X 8 a 2.8 & X 7 b 9.7. Remaining 4 guns retained their position in VILLEVÊQUE	
	31·3·17		Guns from positions in front of TREFCON have been moved to the following position under instructions from OC Infantry: W 9 d 9.8½, W 10 c 4.9, W 10 a 6.3, W 10 a 3½.8	

E. L. Leech Capt
OC 183 M G Coy
31·3·17.

A5834 Wt W4973/M687 750,000 8/16 D. D. & L. Ltd. Forms/C.2118/13.

April. 1917

Vol XI

War. Diary

- of -

183 Machine Gun Coy

Army Form C. 2118.

WAR DIARY
or
~~INTELLIGENCE SUMMARY.~~

(*Erase heading not required.*)

* Instructions regarding War Diaries and Intelligence Summaries are contained in F. S. Regs., Part II. and the Staff Manual respectively. Title pages will be prepared in manuscript.

Place	Date	Hour	Summary of Events and Information	Remarks and references to Appendices
In the field	1/4/17		No 3. Section relieved No 1. Section with 4 guns at VILLEVÈQUE 8 guns from 104 M.G. Coy attached to this company for emergency. 4 guns in reserve at Coy Hqrs at MONCHY-LAGACHE moved up into positions near the line	Location at TREFCON.
	2/4/17.		Guns in position as follows 2 at R28 d 2.3, 2 at R34 b 9.6. 1 at R35 d 5.3 1 at R35 b 5 2½ 1 at R35 b 5 5 1 at R35 b 4 8½ 4 at VILLEVEQUE. Coy Hqrs moved to VILLEVEQUE QM Stores to ~~CAULAINCOURT~~ TREFCON.	MAP 62 C
	3/4/17		The day was marked by some artillery activity & at night MAISSEMY was shelled heavily, whereas on the right hostile artillery activity was practically nil About 1.40 am rifle fire was heard across the river, towards VERMAND	
	4/4/17		8 Guns attached from 104 M-G Coy left this company. 4 guns of 182 M.G. Coy moved up to TREFCON & attached to this Company. Artillery was very quiet during the day, but towards evening increased. Since evening M.G. fire was noticed between 11. pm & 1 am.	
	5/4/17		Artillery fire by enemy on left was normal during the day. Indirect fire was carried out against FRESNOY-LE-PETIT. At 9.30 pm enemy opened heavy fire to the left (Group of 184 Bgde) across the river At 4.45 am an unusual number of Very lights were noticed.	

A5834 Wt. W4973/M687 750,000 8/16 D. D. & L. Ltd. Forms/C.2118/13.

Instructions regarding War Diaries and Intelligence Summaries are contained in F. S. Regs., Part II. and the Staff Manual respectively. Title pages will be prepared in manuscript.

WAR DIARY
or
~~INTELLIGENCE SUMMARY.~~
(Erase heading not required.)

Army Form C. 2118.

183 M.G. Coy

Place	Date	Hour	Summary of Events and Information	Remarks and references to Appendices
In the field	6/4/17		Gun withdrawn from M26 d 9.5 after attack on FRESNOY. At night indirect fire was performed in conjunction with artillery operations on FRESNOY-LE-PETIT and BERTHACOURT. 8 guns of 182 M G Coy assisted on right. The 4 guns cooperated with the infantry, position as follows M32 b 0.9 M26 c 9.0. Direct observation was obtained of exits from village, these being covered. Another gun was at M26 d 9.5 and another at M32 c 8.5. At BERTHAUCOURT in addition to Indirect Fire Programme 4 guns went forward in support of infantry & took up position at M15 c 2.3 & M18 d 5.1 covering approaches & village in enfilade.	Sheets 62 C & 62B. [initials]
	7/4/17		This Company was relieved in the line by 182 M G Coy the Company marching on completion of relief to Billets in MERICOURT.	[initials]
	8/4/17		General cleaning up by men.	[initials]
	9/4/17		Cleaning guns, spare parts & making good etc. & repacking limbers	[initials]

A5834 Wt W4973/M687 750,000 8/16 D. D. & L. Ltd. Forms/C.2118/13.

Army Form C. 2118.

Instructions regarding War Diaries and Intelligence Summaries are contained in F. S. Regs., Part II. and the Staff Manual respectively. Title pages will be prepared in manuscript.

WAR DIARY
or
INTELLIGENCE SUMMARY.
(Erase heading not required.)

Place	Date	Hour	Summary of Events and Information	Remarks and references to Appendices
In the field	10/4/17		Coy moved from BILLET in MERICOURT & marched to ATHIES and took over billets from 106 M.G. Coy	[illegible]
	11/4/17		Unpacking, cleaning gun equipment & general fatigues. 1 Officer & 3 men on aeroplane observation course of IV Corps.	[illegible]
	12/4/17		Coy inspection & equipment, arms, & kit. Deficiencies taken & drill	[illegible]
	13/4/17		Work on ranges. & General Training.	[illegible]
	14/4/17		Training as per programme.	[illegible]
	15/4/17		Coy left in parties for road fatigue. Lecture on anti aircraft measures. Inspection of Transport	[illegible]
	16/4/17		Training as per programme. 2 Guns detached for anti aircraft work at CLARENCY, under direction of IV Corps M.G.O.	[illegible]
	17/4/17		Training as per programme. Range Work	[illegible]
	18/4/17		General Training (Mechanism, Stoppages, open field work.	[illegible]
	19/4/17		General Training	[illegible]
	20/4/17		General Training & packing stores and limbers	[illegible]
	21/4/17		Coy moved from ATHIES to FORRESTE. Hqrs, Stores and Transport in grounds of SUGAR REFINERY.	[illegible]
	22/4/17		Cleaning billets & general sanitation.	[illegible]

A5834 Wt. W4973/M687 750,000 8/16 D. D. & L. Ltd. Forms/C.2118/13.

Instructions regarding War Diaries and Intelligence Summaries are contained in F. S. Regs., Part II. and the Staff Manual respectively. Title pages will be prepared in manuscript.

WAR DIARY
or
~~INTELLIGENCE SUMMARY.~~
(Erase heading not required.)

183 M G Coy

Army Form C. 2118.

Place	Date	Hour	Summary of Events and Information	Remarks and references to Appendices
In the field	23/4/17		Cleaning up still continued, also further Sanitary work	[illegible]
	24/4/17		General Training, and continuation of Sanitation.	[illegible]
	25/4/17		General Training, continuation of Sanitation, also 16 Men and 4 Limbers Reported to Town Major, FORESTE, for Sanitary Work.	[illegible]
	26/4/17		General Training as per programme also 16 Men and 4 Limbers Reported to Town Major, FORÉSTE, for Sanitary Work.	[illegible]
	27/4/17		General Training as per programme – Work on Wagon Lines, clearing away rubbish, etc. Also 16 Men & 4 Limbers reported to Town Major, FORESTE, for futher Sanitary work.	[illegible]
	28/4/17		General Training as per programme	[illegible]
	29/4/17		Church Parades.	[illegible]
	30/4/17		General Training as per programme. 40 Men for working fatigue reported to Divisional H.Q.	[illegible]

30.4.17.

[illegible] Lt.
[illegible] 183 M. G. Coy

A5834 Wt W4973/M687 750,000 8/16 D. D & L. Ltd. Forms/C.2118/13.

May 1917.

Vol 12

War Diary

of

183rd Machine Gun Coy.

WAR DIARY
or
~~INTELLIGENCE SUMMARY.~~
(Erase heading not required.)

Army Form

*Instructions regarding War Diaries and Intelligence Summaries are contained in F. S. Regs., Part II. and the Staff Manual respectively. Title pages will be prepared in manuscript.

183 M. G. Company.

Place	Date	Hour	Summary of Events and Information	Remarks and references to Appendices
In the field	1-5-17		Company relieved 184 M.G. Company in the line - Relief complete by 2-0am. 2-5-17. Artillery on both sides only slightly active. M.G. fire noticed on front of the Brigade on our right. No enemy M.G. fire reported.	
	2-5-17		Enemy artillery active at intervals 7.0am - 11.0am, in right subsection. Short, severe barrage at 3-45 a.m. in region of our front line, FAYET. Artillery quiet on the whole. Some m.g. fire noticed on front of right Brigade during night. Aerial activity on both sides 'lively'. A "blind" bomb was dropped near No 3 Gun position in Outpost Line.	
	3-5-17		<u>Enemy Artillery</u> - below normal. FAYET shelled with 5.9's at 6.0pm. - THREE COTTAGES during day. 4-0am heavy shrapnel barrage on our forward posts, desultory fire continued. <u>Our Artillery</u> - Active at 1-30am. Shoot appeared to be directed by aeroplane. After 5mins rapid fire, a dump appeared to have been fired. <u>M.G. Fire</u> - Normal. <u>Work</u> - Improvement to Section Hqrs. + Gun Positions.	
	4-5-17		Artillery activity during day slight. At night the Enemy put a barrage on our front posts 9-30pm. M.G. fire slight. Aerial activity great. One of our Machines was brought down and fell in ST. QUENTIN 6-30am. Gun position taken over from 182 M.G. Coy. at S.12.a.9.5. Relief complete 12 m.n.	
	5-5-17		Artillery activity during day slight, increased towards evening. On our left, heavy bombardment from both sides between 12-30am. & 1-5 a.m. Indirect fire against Crater + region of M.24.d.4.6. + on Copses in M.30.c. in conjunction with left Brigade between 12-30 & 1-30 a.m. M.G. fire against our front slight.	

A5834 Wt. W4973/M687 750,000 8/16 D. D. & L. Ltd. Forms/C.2118/13.

Army Form C. 2118.

Instructions regarding War Diaries and Intelligence Summaries are contained in F. S. Regs., Part II. and the Staff Manual respectively. Title pages will be prepared in manuscript.

WAR DIARY
or
~~INTELLIGENCE SUMMARY.~~
(Erase heading not required.)

Place	Date	Hour	Summary of Events and Information	Remarks and references to Appendices
In the field.	6-5-17		Artillery activity normal during day. During the night enemy shelling in response to red + green lights. Early part of night our M.G's fired on KILWORTH STICKS, and Enemy works in T.7, retaliatory shelling fell wide. A fire was burning during the whole night in ST. QUENTIN, S. of the Cathedral. Sounds of Transport + trains reported by forward right Section.	
	7-5-17		Slight artillery activity during day - Increased between 9-30 pm & 3.0 a.m. Two of our M.G's fired between 9-30 pm & 10-30 pm on M.30.a.2.0 & M.30.c.5.1. During this time enemy put up many Very Lights. 1-40 a.m. a whistle was heard in direction of CEPY FARM, followed by several explosions.	
	8-5-17		Slight artillery activity. Little enemy M.G. fire. Our M.G's fired from 9.0 to 10-30 pm. on WOOD in M.30.b. & TRACK S.E. No retaliation. Much sniping from CEPY FARM. At 11-45 pm explosions were heard in the farm + one single explosion at 12-15 a.m. Enemy bombed his own wire in front of TWIN COPSE between 10.0 p.m. & M.N.	
	9-5-17		Enemy artillery activity quiet, increased after mid-day. Our Artillery active 9-45 pm. 9-45 pm to 10.5 pm. Four of our M.G's fired on M.30 central + M.30.d. and between 10.0 pm + 12 M.N. on T.7.c. & d, + at M.N. T.13.d. was searched. No retaliation. A sniper succeeded in piercing the barrel casing of our gun in NAMELESS COPSE.	
	10-5-17		Artillery normal till 3-0 pm. when enemy bombarded with heavy shells area between BROWN LINE and HOLNON. Our Artillery opened heavy fire at 4-0 pm. + our M.G's co-operated with Indirect fire on M.36.a and b and M.30.d. lifting as per programme to road in M.30.b. 11.0 pm - 1-30 a.m. our M.G's fired on T.7.	

A5834 Wt. W4973/M687 750,000 8/16 D. D. & L. Ltd. Forms/C.2118/13.

Instructions regarding War Diaries and Intelligence Summaries are contained in F. S. Regs., Part II. and the Staff Manual respectively. Title pages will be prepared in manuscript.

WAR DIARY

~~or~~

~~INTELLIGENCE SUMMARY.~~

(Erase heading not required.)

Army Form C. 2118.

Place	Date	Hour	Summary of Events and Information	Remarks and references to Appendices
In the field	11-5-17		Artillery on both sides active. M.33.d.1.6. severely shelled by enemy. The Gunners were to get away, also 2nd gun teams, which were in same position. Both M.G.s were brought to a safe position. Enemy Aeroplane was driven off by M.G. fire at 7-0 pm. 11-30 pm – 12-30 pm. 4 guns did indirect fire on T.7. drawing heavy m.g. retaliation & some shrapnel. Enemy m.g. – from St. Martin's Church (?), St Quentin – very active 3-30 am.	
	12-5-17.		Artillery quiet. Indirect fire by our m.gs. 1-16 a.m. to 1-40 a.m. & at 1-40 a.m. (programme) on T.7. centre, T.1.a.2.5 – T.1.c.7.5., & KILWORTH STICKS. & trenches in rear. No retaliation. Two large fires seen in ST. QUENTIN.	
	13-5-17		Artillery quiet. Indirect fire by our m.gs. on TOMAHAWK CORSE, tracks and roads in rear, also T.7. no retaliation.	
	14-5-17		Artillery below normal. M.G. Coys of 139 Infantry Regt (French) with our guns during night. Move completed without accident.	
	15-5-17		Artillery normal. 3-0 pm. FRESNOY heavily shelled. 3 COTTAGES shelled intermittently during afternoon. During the day we gave French a demonstration in Indirect fire, target, TOMAHAWK COPSE. Enemy m.g. from direction of BARRACKS, ST. QUENTIN swept our front line & ridge in rear from 9-30 pm. onwards. On the night 15th/16th Company were relieved in the line by 139 ~~Batt.~~ Infy. Regt. (French). Relief complete by 12 m.n. without accident, & moved to billets in GERMAINE.	
	16-5-17		The day was spent in general cleaning up etc.	

A5834 Wt. W4973/M687 750,000 8/16 D. D. & L. Ltd. Forms/C.2118/13.

Instructions regarding War Diaries and Intelligence Summaries are contained in F. S. Regs., Part II. and the Staff Manual respectively. Title pages will be prepared in manuscript.

WAR DIARY

or

INTELLIGENCE SUMMARY.

(Erase heading not required.)

Army Form C. 2118.

Place	Date	Hour	Summary of Events and Information	Remarks and references to Appendices
In the field.	17-5-17		Company moved from GERMAINE & proceeded to billets at CHURCHY nr. NESLE. The route was FORRESTE, DOUILLY, MATIGNY, VOYENNES, NESLE. Left at 7-30 a.m. arrived at 1-0 p.m.	
	18-5-17		Company moved from CURCHY & entrained at NESLE at 7-15 a.m. and detrained at LONGEAU, & proceeded to billets at COISY, arriving there at 2-40 p.m.	
	19-5-17		General Training as per programme	
	20-5-17		Gun Cleaning, & repacking Limbers.	
	21-5-17		Company left COISY & proceeded to billets in BEAUVAL arriving at 1-10 p.m. The route taken was VILLERS BOCAGE, TALMAS, LAHCOGNE.	
	22-5-17		Cleaning Guns, Gun Stores, repacking Limbers & General Cleaning up.	
	23-5-17		Company left BEAUVAL at 7-0 a.m. & proceeded to GRAND RULLECOURT arriving there at 2-20 p.m. Route - DOULLENS, GROUCHES, LUCHEUX.	
	24-5-17		Company left GRAND RULLECOURT at 9-0 a.m. & arrived at DAINVILLE at 3-5 p.m. Route - SOBRIN, SAULTY, enbussed at L'ARBRET, BEAUMETZ.	
	25-5-17		Cleaning of Guns & Gun Stores, Foot Inspection & General cleaning up.	
	26-5-17		General Training as per programme.	
	27-5-17		General Training as per programme.	
	28-5-17		Attack Practices, Revolver Practices, & Range. (M.G.)	
	29-5-17		General Training as per programme.	

A5834 Wt. W4973/M687 750,000 8/16 D. D. & L. Ltd. Forms/C2118/13.

Instructions regarding War Diaries and Intelligence Summaries are contained in F. S. Regs., Part II. and the Staff Manual respectively. Title pages will be prepared in manuscript.

WAR DIARY

~~or~~

~~INTELLIGENCE SUMMARY.~~

(Erase heading not required.)

Army Form C. 2118.

Place	Date	Hour	Summary of Events and Information	Remarks and references to Appendices
In the field	30-5-17		General Training as per programme.	
	31-5-17		General Training as per programme	

E. h. Leech Capt
OC 183 M.G.Coy

A5834 Wt. W4973/M687 750,000 8/16 D. D. & L. Ltd. Forms/C.2118/13.

Vol 13

June 1917.

War Diary

of

183rd Machine Gun Coy.

Instructions regarding War Diaries and Intelligence Summaries are contained in F. S. Regs., Part II. and the Staff Manual respectively. Title pages will be prepared in manuscript.

WAR DIARY

~~or~~

~~INTELLIGENCE SUMMARY.~~

(Erase heading not required.)

Army Form C. 2118.

183rd Machine Gun Company.

Place	Date	Hour	Summary of Events and Information	Remarks and references to Appendices
~~In the Field~~ TILLOY	1-6-17		Company relieved 184 M. G. Coy. in Support at TILLOY. Left DAINVILLE at 2-45 p.m and arrived at TILLOY at 5-0pm. The moring was spent in packing limbers and cleaning Billets.	
"	2-6-17		General Training as per programme, also work on dugouts.	
"	3-6-17		General Training as per programme, work on dugouts, and at 9-0pm. 30 men reported at 184 Bde Hqrs for work.	
"	4-6-17		General Training as per programme, work on dugouts, and at 9-30pm. 20 men reported at 184 Bde Hqrs for work.	
"	5-6-17		General Training as per programme, work on dugouts, and at 9-30 pm. 30 men reported at 184 Bde Hqrs for work.	
"	6-6-17		General Training as per programme, work on dugouts, and at 9-30pm. 25 men reported at 184 Bde Hqrs for work on dugouts and m.g. emplacements.	
"	7-6-17		General Training as per programme, and at 9-30pm. a working party of 25 men reported to 184 Bde Hqrs. for work on dugouts etc.	
"	8-6-17		General Training as per programme, also working party reported at 9-30pm to 184 Brigade Hqrs.	
"	9-6-17		General Training as per programme.	
"	10-6-17		Cleaning & tidying up Billets, dugouts, etc, and surroundings.	

A5834 Wt. W4973/M687 750,000 8/16 D. D. & L. Ltd. Forms/C.2118/13.

Army Form C. 2118.

Instructions regarding War Diaries and Intelligence Summaries are contained in F. S. Regs., Part II. and the Staff Manual respectively. Title pages will be prepared in manuscript.

WAR DIARY
or
~~INTELLIGENCE SUMMARY.~~

(Erase heading not required.)

183 Machine Gun Coy.

Place	Date	Hour	Summary of Events and Information	Remarks and references to Appendices
~~[illegible]~~	10·6·17		Also at 10·25pm Company left TILLOY & proceeded via FAUB ST SAUVEUR, ARRAS, FBG D'AMIENS, DAINVILLE, BERNEVILLE, to SIMENCOURT, arriving at 2-10 AM 11-6-17.	
SIMENCOURT.	11·6·17		General Cleaning up.	
"	12·6·17		General Training as per programme.	
"	13·6·17		General Training as per programme.	
"	14·6·17		General Training as per programme.	
"	15·6·17		General Training as per programme.	
"	16·6·17		General Training as per programme.	
"	17·6·17		Church Parades.	
"	18·6·17		General Training as per programme.	
"	19·6·17		General Training as per programme.	
"	20·6·17		The day was held as a general holiday; Company Sports were held in the afternoon, and in the evening the Brigade Sports were held.	
"	21·6·17		Limbers were packed, and billets were thoroughly cleaned. At 4-30 pm. the Transport left SIMENCOURT and arrived at REBREUVE AREA @ 9-0 pm.	
NEULETTE	22·6·17		The Company left SIMENCOURT at 8·18 am, marched to GOUY-EN-ARTOIS & entrained there at 9-45 am. Detrained at HESDIN at 3·15 pm. & marched via LE PARCQ to NEULETTE arriving there at 6-10 pm. Transport left REBREUVE AREA at 7·30 am. and arrived at NEULETTE at 9-15 pm.	

A5834 Wt. W4973/M687 750,000 8/16 D. D. & L. Ltd. Forms/C.2118/13.

Instructions regarding War Diaries and Intelligence Summaries are contained in F. S. Regs., Part II. and the Staff Manual respectively. Title pages will be prepared in manuscript.

WAR DIARY
or
~~INTELLIGENCE SUMMARY.~~
(Erase heading not required.)

Army Form C. 2118.

183 Machine Gun Coy.

Place	Date	Hour	Summary of Events and Information	Remarks and references to Appendices
23-6-17			The day was spent in cleaning guns + gun stores, + limbers.	
~~[illegible]~~	24-6-17		Kit & Equipment Inspection.	
NEULETTE.	25-6-17		General Training.	
	26-6-17		General Training.	
	27-6-17		General Training.	
	28-6-17		General Training.	
	29-6-17		General Training	
	30-6-17		Brigade Horse Show, at WILLEMAN.	
			30-6-17 D. H. Leck Capt. O.C. 183 M. G. Coy.	

A5834 Wt W4973/M687 750,000 8/16 D. D. & L. Ltd. Forms/C.2118/13.

183 Machine Gun Coy

Vol 14

WAR DIARY.

JULY 1917.

Instructions regarding War Diaries and Intelligence Summaries are contained in F. S. Regs., Part II. and the Staff Manual respectively. Title pages will be prepared in manuscript.

WAR DIARY

or

~~INTELLIGENCE SUMMARY.~~

(Erase heading not required.)

Army Form C. 2118.

183 M. G. Coy.

Place	Date	Hour	Summary of Events and Information	Remarks and references to Appendices
NEULETTE	1-7-17	–	The Divisional General presented ribands to Recipients of medals, at WILLEMAN.	BM
do.	2-7-17	–	General Training as per programme.	BM
do.	3-7-17	–	General Training as per programme.	BM
do.	4-7-17	–	General Training as per programmes	BM
do.	5-7-17	–	General Training (Firing on long range at WAIL).	BM
do.	6-7-17	–	General Training as per programme.	BM
do.	7-7-17	–	General Training as per programme.	BM
do.	8-7-17	-	Church Parades	BM
do.	9-7-17	-	General Training as per programme.	BM
do.	10-7-17	–	General Training as per programme.	BM
do.	11-7-17	–	General Training as per programme	BM
do.	12-7-17	–	General Training as per programme	BM
do.	13-7-17	–	General Training. @ 6-0 pm. Church Service.	BM
do.	14-7-17	-	General Training.	BM
do.	15-7-17	–	Church Parades.	BM
do.	16-7-17	-	General Training for ½ Coy. ½ Coy. took part in Battalion Trench attack Scheme.	BM
do	17-7-17	-	General Training as per programme.	BM
do.	18-7-17	-	Bombing Instruction under Brigade Bombing Officer.	BM

A5831 Wt W4973/M687 750,000 8/16 D. D. & L. Ltd. Forms/C.2118/13.

Army Form C. 2118.

Instructions regarding War Diaries and Intelligence Summaries are contained in F. S. Regs., Part II. and the Staff Manual respectively. Title pages will be prepared in manuscript.

WAR DIARY
or
INTELLIGENCE SUMMARY.
(Erase heading not required.)

183 M.G. Coy.

Place	Date	Hour	Summary of Events and Information	Remarks and references to Appendices
NEULETTE	19-7-17	–	Bombing Instruction under Brigade Bombing Officer.	B.L.
do	20-7-17	–	Bombing Instruction under Brigade Bombing Officer, at BLANGERMONT.	B.L.
do	21-7-17	–	General Training - Barrage Fire ~~at~~ on WAIL - FILLIEVRES Road.	B.L.
do	22-7-17	–	Church Parades.	B.L.
do	23-7-17	–	Cleaning & Packing Limbers, & general cleaning up preparatory to moving.	B.L.
do	24-7-17	–	Left NEULETTE at 7-45 am. & reach ECOIVRES at 11-10 am. Route HUMIERES, BEAUVOIS, CROISETTE.	B.L.
ECOIVRES	25-7-17	–	Left ECOIVRES at 7-45 pm. & entrained at PETIT HOUVIN at 8-20 pm. route direct.	B.L.
PETIT HOUVIN	26-7-17	–	Detrained at ESQUELBECQ. at 2-15 am. and arrived at ZEGGERS CAPPEL at 11-10 am. Route direct.	B.L.
	27-7-17 28-7-17 29-7-17 30-7-17 31-7-17		General Training as per programme.	B.L.

B. Leck Capt
O.C. 183 M.G. Coy.

31-7-17

A5834 Wt. W4973/M687 750,000 8/16 D. D. & L. Ltd. Forms/C.2118/13.

August 1917

Vol 15

War Diary

of

183 Machine Gun Coy

Army Form C. 2118.

WAR DIARY
or
INTELLIGENCE SUMMARY.
(Erase heading not required.)

Instructions regarding War Diaries and Intelligence Summaries are contained in F. S. Regs., Part II. and the Staff Manual respectively. Title pages will be prepared in manuscript.

183 M.G. Coy.

Place	Date	Hour	Summary of Events and Information	Remarks and references to Appendices
ZEGGERS CAPPEL AREA	1-8-17 to 14-8-17		General Training as per programme	HAZEBROUCK 5A 1/100,000
	15-8-17		Company left ZEGGERS CAPPEL AREA at 5.40 am & entrained at ESQUELBECQ at 6.20 am. Detrained at POPERINGHE at 12.0 noon & arrived in camp, ½ mile S.E. of POPERINGHE at 1.40 pm.	
	16-8-17		Left POPERINGHE area at 9.15 a.m. & arrived in Camp (GOLDFISH CHATEAU) YPRES N. at 11.40 a.m. Route, POPERINGHE STATION, VLAMERTINGHE.	
	17-8-17		Preparing to go into the line.	
	18-8-17		Two sections left GOLDFISH CHATEAU and proceeded to billets near VLAMERTINGHE arriving at 8.0 am.	
	19-8-17		at 4.0 am. The two sections left at GOLDFISH CHATEAU relieved 107 M.G. Coy in the line. Relief was effected without incident. 4 guns PIMMERN REDOUBT. 4 guns BANK FM	
WIELJE	20-8-17		Enemy shelled vicinity of BANK FM 4 AM - 8 AM. 3 casualties. Enemy shell Bde sector	FREZENBURG 1/10,000.

A5834 Wt. W4973/M687 750,000 8/16 D. D. & L. Ltd. Forms/C.2118/13.

Instructions regarding War Diaries and Intelligence Summaries are contained in F. S. Regs., Part II. and the Staff Manual respectively. Title pages will be prepared in manuscript.

WAR DIARY
~~or~~
~~INTELLIGENCE~~ SUMMARY.
(*Erase heading not required.*)

Army Form C. 2118.

183 Machine Gun Coy.

Place	Date	Hour	Summary of Events and Information	Remarks and references to Appendices
~~21-8-17~~ WIELTJE	21-8-17		Attempt made to take BORRY Fm unsuccessful. preparations made for barrage fire. Ammunition taken up to BANK Fm on mules.	FREZENBURG 1/10000.
"	~~21-8-17~~		Preparations for attack. Fire positions fitted with T bases, ammunition dumps formed. Enemy shelling severe at times. 4 guns from POMMERN move to BANK Fm. 8 guns move from GOLD FISH CHAU to line. Take up positions in CAPRICORN TR.	[illegible]
	22-8-17		4.45 AM barrage guns (16 guns) opened up and carried on firing on barrage lines for 1 hr. 40 min. 130,000 rds were fired. Enemy retaliation not heavy. a concentrated shoot made on WARST Fm at 10 AM 32,000 rds. Bde did not take final objective, but took up the line POND Fm - SOMME - HILL 35.	
	23-8-17		183 Inf. Bde relieved 184 Bde. M.G.C. not relieved. guns still situated in Barrage positions. SOS line barraged at 9 AM, 12 noon, 4 PM & 6 PM in answer to SOS signals. Ammunition taken up by pack mules at night.	[illegible]
	24-8-17		Enemy counter attack on JEW HILL but was held off by M.G. fire (barrage fire). Guns situated as follows 4 guns (184 Coy) JEW HILL 2 guns (184) SOMME 2 guns (182) CONTTR 16 guns (183) CAPRICORN TR - BANK Fm. MAP FREZENBERG 1/10000. SOS lines fired on twice during the night - answer to SOS signals. 8 guns relieved by 8 guns 182 ~~relieved~~ during the night. 8 guns move to GOLDFISH CHAU	[illegible]

A5834 Wt. W4973/M687 750,000 8/16 D. D. & L. Ltd. Forms/C.2118/13.

Instructions regarding War Diaries and Intelligence Summaries are contained in F. S. Regs., Part II. and the Staff Manual respectively. Title pages will be prepared in manuscript.

WAR DIARY
or
~~INTELLIGENCE SUMMARY.~~
(Erase heading not required.)

Army Form C. 2118.

183 M.G. Coy.

Place	Date	Hour	Summary of Events and Information	Remarks and references to Appendices
~~25-8-17~~ WIELTJE	25·8·17		A line of dug-outs D13.c.18 were occupied and wired. Operations were confined to severe sniping, principally in neighbourhood of SPREE & POND Fms. M.G. fire was fairly active at night	FREZENBURG. 1/10,000.
"	26·8·17		Preparations for an attack for 27th. 8 guns already in barrage positions, extra ammunition taken up. Enemy quieter, less artillery fire	E.L.
"	27-8-17		At 2PM 183 Bde made an attack. Weather conditions were very bad it having rained hard through out the night. 8 guns fired on a barrage line D8c30 95 D8c 20.00 and searched 300ˣ down reverse slope. Guns ceased firing at 4.30 AM Inf. did not obtain objective, it being almost impossible for men to move in the mud.	
	28·8·17		Remaining 8 guns moved out by 4 AM to VLAMERTINGHE to reorganize 8 guns already out moved into the line remaining in reserve at WIELTJE.	E.L.
	29-8-17		8 guns in reserve at WIELTJE moved out of the line. The whole Coy at VLAMERTINGHE reorganizing	
VLAMERTINGHE	30·8·17		Generally reorganizing, cleaning up etc	
	31-8-17		Generally re-organizing, cleaning up, etc.	

E.L. Leech Capt

31-8-17.

O.C. 183 M.G. Coy.

A5834 Wt. W4973/M687 750,000 8/16 D. D. & L. Ltd. Forms/C.2118/13.

Sepr 1917

Vol 16

War Diary

of

183rd Machine Gun Coy.

Instructions regarding War Diaries and Intelligence Summaries are contained in F. S. Regs., Part II. and the Staff Manual respectively. Title pages will be prepared in manuscript.

WAR DIARY
or
~~INTELLIGENCE SUMMARY.~~
(Erase heading not required.)

Army Form C. 2118.

183 Machine Gun Coy.

Place	Date	Hour	Summary of Events and Information	Remarks and references to Appendices
VLAMERTINGHE Nr YPRES	1-9-17 2-9-17		Re-organization & Resting.	FREZENBERG 1/10000.
	3-9-17		8 guns relieved 8 guns of 184 M.G. Coy. at POMMERN (1) JASPER Fm (3) C.30.a.25.65 (4). Relief Completed without incident.	
	4-9-17		Operations. Enemy shelled vicinity of JASPER Fm close to gun positions. 30,000 carried up to vicinity of UHLAN Fm where position are under construction for Barrage fire.	
	5-9-17		8 guns went up the line but were sent back immediately. Owing to operations being cancelled. Enemy aeroplanes bombed vicinity of Transport lines near VLAMERTINGHE.	
	6-9-17		Normal no operations. Guns did harassing fire on enemy tracks around HILL 35 - about 4000 rds being fired. Enemy Artillery shell ~~guns~~ Artillery in ST JEAN with mustard gas causing casualties. Gas shells in vicinity of JASPER & UHLAN Fm additional 38,000 rds carried up to above farms.	
	7-9-17		Artillery activity normal except for short bombardment by the enemy of STEEN BECK VALLEY at 5-15 pm. During the night enemy shelled usual areas from 10.0 pm to 4-0 am. Very lights normal. Enemy's fell behind crest of Hill 35.	

A5834 Wt. W4973/M687 750,000 8/16 D. D. & L. Ltd. Forms/C.2118/12.

Instructions regarding War Diaries and Intelligence Summaries are contained in F. S. Regs., Part II. and the Staff Manual respectively. Title pages will be prepared in manuscript.

WAR DIARY

~~or~~

~~INTELLIGENCE~~ ~~SUMMARY.~~

(Erase heading not required.)

Army Form C. 2118.

183 M.G. Coy.

Place	Date	Hour	Summary of Events and Information	Remarks and references to Appendices
WEILTJE	7-9-17	-	E.A. were heard dropping bombs on back areas at 10-0pm also on WEILTJE. 8 guns relieve 8 guns of 182 M.G. Coy.:- 2 at POND Fm 1 SOMME. 4 guns which were to take up position at C.12.d.40-35 did not do so as troops were withdrawn prior to operations tomorrow (8-9-17)	
"	8-9-17	-	8 Guns 184 M.G. Coy. relieved 8 of ours as follows:- 1 at POMMERN 3 at JASPER Fm, 4 at C.30.a.25.65. These 8 guns proceeded to Transport Lines.	
"	9-9-17	-	4 Guns moved up the line, two took up positions on JEW HILL, the other two remaining in junction of CALL RESERVE and ST. JULIEN ROAD.	
"	10-9-17	-	The two guns left at junction of CALL RESERVE & ST. JULIEN ROAD moved up to JEW HILL to reinforce the two guns there.	
	11-9-17		Inter-section relief. Four guns from POND FARM were relieved by 4 guns from Transport Lines.	
	12-9-17		On the night 12th/13th Coy. was relieved by 184 M.G. Coy. Relief completed by 11-0 pm.	
	13-9-17		Left VLAMERTINGHE at 9-30 am. and proceeded to Camp S.E. of POPERINGHE, arriving there at 10-45 am. Route direct.	
	14-9-17		Left POPERINGHE at 8-40 am. & proceeded to WATOU No 2 AREA arriving there at 11-50 am. Route direct.	
	15-9-17 16-9-17 17-9-17		General cleaning & reorganization.	

A5834 Wt. W4973/M687 750,000 8/16 D. D. & L. Ltd. Forms/C.2118/13.

Army Form C. 2118.

WAR DIARY
or
~~INTELLIGENCE SUMMARY.~~
(Erase heading not required.)

Instructions regarding War Diaries and Intelligence Summaries are contained in F. S. Regs., Part II. and the Staff Manual respectively. Title pages will be prepared in manuscript.

183 M.G. Coy.

Place	Date	Hour	Summary of Events and Information	Remarks and references to Appendices
WATOU	18-9-17		Left WATOU No. 2 AREA at 10-0 a.m. and proceeded to billet on CASSEL - WORMHOUDT ROAD, 4 Kilos from WORMHOUDT.	[initials]
WORMHOUDT	19-9-17		Left WORMHOUDT & marched direct to CASSEL STATION & entrained at 11-11 a.m. and detrained at ARRAS at 7-10 p.m. and marched to SIMENCOURT reaching there at 10-35 p.m. Route; ARRAS, ARRAS-DOULLENS ROAD, BERNEVILLE.	[initials]
SIMENCOURT	20-9-17		General Training and cleaning up.	[initials]
"	21-9-17			
"	22-9-17		Coy. left SIMENCOURT at 10-0 a.m. and proceeded to ST GEORGE'S Camp, ST NICHOLAS, arriving at 1-45 p.m., Route: BERNEVILLE, ARRAS-DOULLENS ROAD, ARRAS, ST NICHOLAS.	[initials]
	23-9-17		Relieved 50th M.G. Coy. in the line, GREENLAND HILL Sector, relief completed by 10-15 P.M. without incident. Gun positions (27) H.6.a.4.2. (23A) H.12.b.7.7. (23) H.12.b.8.5 (16) I.1.a.5.4. (26) H.6.b.4.2. (25) H.6.d.5.9. (24A) H.6.d.5.7. (24) H.6.d.5.0. (14) I.1.b.7.5. (8) I.1.c.7.7. (13) I.7.a.8.7. (12) I.7.b.2.4. (6) I.7.b.4.2. (6A) I.7.b.4.7. (15) I.1.a.6.2. (7) I.7.b.7.9. (Refce. Map. T. 18 Ed. 2. 1/10.000). The night was quiet.	
	~~24-9-17~~		at 4.15 a.m. enemy opened vigorous fire with T.M's. & shells of front line of Bde. on right. Our M.G's. carried out indirect fire as follows:-	[initials]

Gun position	Target	No. of Rds.	Time
H.6.a.4.2.	I.3.a.2.4. × roads	2,000.	9-0 pm 23-9-17 to 6-0 Am. 24-9-17.
H.6.d.5.0.	I.8.b.4.4 I.9. central	3,000	do.
H.6.d.5.7.	I.2.d.6.5 I.3.a.2.4	3,000	do.

A5834 Wt W4973/M687 750,000 8/16 D. D. & L. Ltd. Forms/C.2118/13.

Instructions regarding War Diaries and Intelligence Summaries are contained in F. S. Regs., Part II. and the Staff Manual respectively. Title pages will be prepared in manuscript.

WAR DIARY
or
INTELLIGENCE SUMMARY.
(Erase heading not required.)

Army Form C. 2118.

183 M.G. Coy.

Place	Date	Hour	Summary of Events and Information	Remarks and references to Appendices
	24-9-17		Enemy shelled CHILI AV. at intervals during the day. at 7-0 p.m. COSTA CALDRON + top end of CHILI were heavily shelled by enemy for 25 mins. 4-30 to 6-0 p.m. our left sub. section, front line, was bombarded by heavy T.M's. Our M.G's fired as under:-	

Gun.	Target	Rounds.	Time.
A.A.G. 23a.	E.A.	500	12-0 noon
A.A.G. 24.	E.A.	250	12-0 noon
24.	I.3.a.2.4 / I.2.d.6.5	1000 / 1000	9-0 pm to 5-0 am / do.
23a.	I.3.a.2.4 / I.2.d.6.5	1000 / 1000	do
24a.	E.A.	500	12-30 p.m.
27.	I.8.b.4.4	2000	9-0 pm. to 4-0 A.m.
25.	I.9. Central	2000	do.
	Total	9250	

Enemy working party seen working on GREENLAND HILL but dispersed by our M.G's. 9-15 p.m. enemy bombed his own wire for 20 mins, and later between 12 + 1 a.m.

25-9-17 Enemy Artillery, quiet. CIVIL AV. + CHICKEN RES. received attention at about 3-15 p.m. L.T.M's. were dropped between 5 + 7 p.m. around CLAIN' ALLEY + junction of CRY and CHARLIE Spt. Between 4 + 5 a.m. a few more were put over. E.M.G's fired on our wire + support line. Our M.G's. at 12 noon fired on E.A. Indirect fire as follows:-

Gun	Target	Rds. fired	Time
25.	I.3.a.2.4 / I.2.d.6.5	1500 / 2000	9 pm to 4-0 am.
26	I.9. Central	1500	do.
23a.	I-8.b.4.4.	1500	do
23.			do.
	Total	6500	

A5834 Wt. W4973/M687 750,000 8/16 D. D. & L. Ltd. Forms/C.2118/13.

Instructions regarding War Diaries and Intelligence Summaries are contained in F. S. Regs., Part II. and the Staff Manual respectively. Title pages will be prepared in manuscript.

WAR DIARY
or
~~INTELLIGENCE SUMMARY.~~
(Erase heading not required.)

Army Form C. 2118.

183 M.G. Coy.

Place	Date	Hour	Summary of Events and Information	Remarks and references to Appendices
	26-9-17		Enemy Artillery. fairly active during afternoon. Their T.M's dropped some around CONRAD between 2-30pm. & 3-15pm. E.M.G's. active against our aeroplanes between 7pm & 12 mn. & along parapet of CORK SUPPORT. Our M.G's carried out fire as follows.	
			Gun / Target / Rds. / Time.	
			A.A. Cork Spt. / E.A. / 100 / 6-40pm.	
			25. H.6.d.5.9. / I.3.b.5.0. / 1500 / 9-0pm to 4-0am.	
			6. H.1.b.4.3. / I.9. Central / 1500 / do.	
			23a. H.12.b.6.7. / I.3.a.2.4. / 2000 / do.	
			24. H.6.d.5.0 / I.2.d.6.5 / 2000 / do	
			Total 7000	
			Work. revetting, deepening & improving trenches around emplacements.	
	27-9-17		Enemy Artillery. COSTA, CALDRON, CHILI & CHALK Res. were lightly shelled during the morning, and again in the afternoon. CHALK RES. & CHILI AV. were shelled with gas shells at about 10-0pm. E.T.M's. sent over 12 minnies between CORK SUPPORT & front line. E.M.G.S. fairly active through the night. Our M.G's. A gun was laid on a party which appeared at dusk in the direction of WEED Trench & during the night this area was searched & traversed. 1500 rds. expended.	
			Gun / Target / Rds. / Time.	
			25 / I.3.a.2.4. / 1000 / 8 to 10 pm.	
			26 / do / 1000 / do.	
			23A. / WEED TRENCH / 750 / 9 to 4 am.	
			24 / do / 750 / do.	
			Total 3500	
			Work – Revetting and improving trenches.	

A5834 Wt. W4973/M687 750,000 8/16 D. D. & L. Ltd. Forms/C.2118/12.

Instructions regarding War Diaries and Intelligence Summaries are contained in F. S. Regs., Part II. and the Staff Manual respectively. Title pages will be prepared in manuscript.

WAR DIARY or ~~INTELLIGENCE SUMMARY.~~

(Erase heading not required.)

Army Form C. 2118.

183 M.G. Coy.

Place	Date	Hour	Summary of Events and Information	Remarks and references to Appendices
FAMPOUX	28.9.17		Enemy Artillery fairly active around COSTA, CALDRON, CHILI + CHALK during the morning. Their T.M's. retaliated to our shoot at 7-15. Our M.G's cooperated in the shoot at 7-15 on WEASEL + junction of WEASEL + WAVY. 2000 rds expended.	[illegible]

Gun	Target	Rds.	Time.
25	I.2.d.65.50.	500	7-15 pm
26	do	500	do.
23A	I.2.c.70.15	500	do.
24	I.2.d.60-50.	500	do.
25	I.8.b.45.45	1500	9.0pm to 4-0am
26	do	1500	do
23	WEED TR.	1000	do
23A	do	1500	do
24	do	1500	do.
	Total	9,000	

Place	Date	Hour	Summary of Events and Information	Remarks and references to Appendices
do.	29.9.17		Enemy Artillery - quiet during morning. CHALK RES shelled in afternoon. Reserve front lines bombarded heavily from 1-0 to 1-45 am. Enemy T.M's. joined in this bombardment. Our M.G's. fired on their S.O.S. line from 1-0 to 1-45 am. 11,000 rds. Indirect fire as under.	[illegible]

Gun	Target	Rds.	Time.
25	I.3.a.20.40.	1000	9-0pm to 4-0 am. intermittently.
26	I.2.d.65.55.	1250	
23a	I.8.b.45.45.	1000	do
24	WEED TR.	1000	
	Total.	4250	

A fire was noticed burning fiercely behind enemy's line, bearing 75° mag. from I.1a.5.4.

A5834 Wt. W4973/M687 750,000 8/16 D. D. & L. Ltd. Forms/C.2118/13.

Instructions regarding War Diaries and Intelligence Summaries are contained in F. S. Regs., Part II. and the Staff Manual respectively. Title pages will be prepared in manuscript.

WAR DIARY

or

~~INTELLIGENCE SUMMARY.~~

(Erase heading not required.)

Army Form C. 2118.

183 M.G. Coy.

Place	Date	Hour	Summary of Events and Information	Remarks and references to Appendices
FAMPOUX	30-9-17		Enemy Artillery - quiet. T.M.S. quiet. Enemy M.G's. normal. Our M.G's cooperated in shoot at 2-30pm. Rds. 4500. Indirect fire as follows	

Gun.	Target	Rds. fired	Time
23A	WEASEL TR	1000	230 p.m.
24	"	1000	
24A	I.3.a. 90.40	750	
25	"	750	
26	Cugot AV. to C.26.d.	500	
27	"	500	
23	I.8.b.45.45	1000	9-0 pm to 4-30 AM.
23A	"	1000	
24	I.3.a.70.40	1000	
25	I.8.b.45.45	2000	
26	I.9. central	2000	

E.A's. were unusually active, two of our planes were brought down one at 12 noon in our lines & one at 12.15 in enemy's lines.
Work continued under R.E's.

30/9/17

[signature]
for O.C., 183 M.G. Coy.

A5834 Wt. W4973/M687 750,000 8/16 D. D. & L. Ltd. Forms/C.2118/13.

Vol 17

October 1917

War Diary

of

183rd Machine Gun Coy

Instructions regarding War Diaries and Intelligence Summaries are contained in F. S. Regs., Part II. and the Staff Manual respectively. Title pages will be prepared in manuscript.

WAR DIARY

~~or~~

~~INTELLIGENCE SUMMARY.~~

(Erase heading not required.)

Army Form C. 2118.

183 Machine Gun Coy.

Place	Date	Hour	Summary of Events and Information	Remarks and references to Appendices
GREEN-LAND HILL.	1-10-17		Enemy Artillery quiet during the whole 24 hours. Enemy T.M.S fired on CORK SUPPORT + CHICKEN RESERVE between 2-15 + 2-30 pm. Their M.G's were normal. Our M.G's fired between 9-0 pm + 4-30 am. on the usual night targets, 6750 rds. also cooperated with Artillery shoots, 3800 rds.	
	2-10-17		Enemy Artillery normal. Our M.G's. fired on usual tracks + communication trenches, 11500 rds.	
	3-10-17		Enemy Artillery above normal. Enemy T.M.S. quiet. We carried out I.F. on tracks, communication trenches, junctions of trenches, etc, 10,000 rds. Work - Revetting + improving trenches, etc.	
	4-10-17		Coy. was relieved in the line by 184 M.G. Coy. Relief completed by 12-0 noon. Coy. proceeded to reserve Camp, ST. NICHOLAS.	
ST. NICHOLAS.	5-10-17		General cleaning, etc.	
	6-10-17		General training as per programme.	
	7-10-17			
	8-10-17			
	9-10-17			
	10-10-17			
	11-10-17			
	12-10-17			
	13-10-17			
	14-10-17			

A5834 Wt. W4973/M687 750,000 8/16 D. D. & L. Ltd. Forms/C.2118/13.

Army Form C. 2118.

Instructions regarding War Diaries and Intelligence Summaries are contained in F. S. Regs., Part II. and the Staff Manual respectively. Title pages will be prepared in manuscript.

WAR DIARY
~~or~~
~~INTELLIGENCE SUMMARY.~~

(Erase heading not required.)

183 Machine Gun Coy

Place	Date	Hour	Summary of Events and Information	Remarks and references to Appendices
FAMPOUX	15.10.17		Coy. relieved 182 M.G. Coy. in CHEMICAL WORKS SECTOR. Relief complete without incident by ~~[illegible]~~ 3-45 p.m. E. Artillery quiet. E.T.M's normal. E.M.G's active during night on tracks near SINGLE ARCH + CORDITE TRENCH. During hours of darkness our M.G's fired on tracks, etc. 7,000 rds.	[initials]
	16.10.17		Enemy Artillery quiet, T.M's. quiet, M.G's very active at night. Our M.G's. 2250 rds fired on E.A's. I.F. was carried out during the night on enemy tracks + communication trenches. 12,000 rds.	[initials]
	17.10.17		Enemy Artillery, normal. FAMPOUX shelled during the day. T.M's. quiet. E.M.G's 5.45 pm to 9-0 pm. very active on front system, otherwise normal. Our M.G's engaged E.A's during the day, + at night I.F. was carried out on enemy tracks + communication trenches, 8,000 rds. Work - constructing new barrage position. + repairing trenches + M.G. E's.	[initials]
	18.10.17		Enemy Artillery. Fairly active during the day. T.M's. quiet. M.G's. normal. Our M.G's. fired 3550 rds on E.A. During the night harassing fire was carried out on enemy tracks + C.T's., 8000 rds.	[initials]
	19.10.17		Enemy Artillery normal. T.M's. quiet. M.G's. fairly active during the night. Our M.G's carried out usual harassing fire. 8000 rds.	[initials]
	20.10.17		Enemy Artillery - normal. T.M's. normal. M.G's active during the night. Our M.G's carried out usual harassing fire on tracks, etc 8000. Lachrymatory gas was reported, but only very slight.	[initials]

A5834 Wt. W4973/M687 750,000 8/16 D. D. & L. Ltd. Forms/C.2118/13.

Instructions regarding War Diaries and Intelligence Summaries are contained in F. S. Regs., Part II. and the Staff Manual respectively. Title pages will be prepared in manuscript.

WAR DIARY
or
~~INTELLIGENCE SUMMARY.~~
(Erase heading not required.)

Army Form C. 2118.

183 M.G. Coy.

Place	Date	Hour	Summary of Events and Information	Remarks and references to Appendices
FAMPOUX	21-10-17		Enemy Artillery active between 6.0 pm & 1.0 am. CHEMICAL WORKS receiving special attention. Gas shells fell near Reserve Line at 5-30 pm & at 9-15 pm. T.M'S. active at intervals. M.G'S. active on front system. Our M.G'S. I.F. on tracks & trenches, 6,000 rds.	[initials]
	22-10-17		Enemy Artillery - quiet. T.M'S. active on front system. M.G'S. active. CINEMA TRENCH & CADIZ RES. received special attention. Our M.G's carried out ~~I.F.~~ Indirect fire on tracks & trenches, 4,000 rds.	[initials]
	23-10-17		Enemy Artillery - fairly active the whole 24 hrs. T.M'S. quiet. M.G's active during night. Our M.G's fired 20,000 rds barrage in support of raid by Brigade on left. Indirect fire on tracks, 2000 rds.	[initials]
	24-10-17		Enemy Artillery - very active during raid by our Brigade. M.G's very active 24 hrs. Our Barrage Battery (M.G's) fired 43,000 rds in support of raid between 2.30 to 4-10 pm & between 9-30 & 9.55 p.m. 5,00 rds were fired at E.A.	[initials]
	25-10-17		Enemy Artillery quiet. M.G's active during night. T.M'S. quieter than usual. Our M.G'S carried out I.F. on tracks communication trenches etc. during the night. 4,000 rds.	[initials]
	26-10-17		Enemy Artillery, Normal. T.M'S. quiet. M.G'S. active at night. Our M.G's carried out I.F. on usual tracks, etc. 4 000 rds.	[initials]
	27-10-17		Enemy Artillery - very active. T.M'S. active during morning. M.G'S. usual activity during night. Our M.G's. were laid on barrage lines in expectation of an enemy raid, which did not materialise. I.F. carried out as usual. 6,500 rds.	[initials]

A5834 Wt. W4973/M687 750,000 8/16 D. D. & L. Ltd. Forms/C.2118/13.

Instructions regarding War Diaries and Intelligence Summaries are contained in F. S. Regs., Part II. and the Staff Manual respectively. Title pages will be prepared in manuscript.

WAR DIARY

~~or~~

~~INTELLIGENCE SUMMARY.~~

(*Erase heading not required.*)

Army Form C. 2118.

183 M.G. Coy.

Place	Date	Hour	Summary of Events and Information	Remarks and references to Appendices
FAMPOUX	28-10-17		Enemy Artillery quiet, T.M'S. normal. M.G's. normal. Our M.G's. fired 250 rds at E.A. I.F. on usual targets 3500 rds.	[initials]
	29-10-17		Enemy Artillery Normal. T.M's normal. M.G's. active during early morning. Our M.G. Barrage Battery fired 13,000 rds in support of a raid by our Brigade. 4000 rds were fired by other guns on the usual Indirect fire targets.	[initials]
	30-10-17		Enemy Artillery very active on back areas. T.M'S. quiet. M.G's - normal. Our M.G'S. carried out Indirect Fire on enemy tracks + C.T'S. during the night 14000 rds.	[initials]
	31-10-17		Enemy Artillery - Fairly active. T.M's. more active than usual. M.G's normal. Our M.G's. (Barrage Battery) fired 4,000 rds. in conjunction with 18 pdr. Barrage at 4-0 am. I.F. was carried out during the night on enemy tracks + C.Ts. 6,000 rds. A great deal of aerial Activity during the morning.	[initials]

[signature] Lt
for O.C., 183 M.G. Coy.

A5834 Wt. W4973/M687 750,000 8/16 D. D. & L. Ltd. Forms/C.2118/13.

S.C.4178

21.12.17.

Headquarters,
61st. Division

Forwarded with reference to 61st. Division No.Q 36

dated 20.12.17.

G.E.W. Bowyer, Capt.
for Brig.Gen.
Commanding 183rd. Infantry Brigade.

B.H.Q.
21.12.17.

D.A.G
3rd Echelon.

War Diary of 183 M.G. Coy. for November 1917 herewith

H. C. [illegible] Lt. Col.
for Maj. Gen.
Comdg. 61st Division

D.H.Q.
26.12.17

To H Qrs (Rear) 183 Infantry Brigade

From OC 183 M G C (Rear)

Reference S C 4178 20-12-17

Herewith one copy of War Diary for Nov. According to our records, this should have been sent off on Nov 30th in the usual way, but evidently it has been mislaid

E E Wardle Lt
for OC 183 M G C

61

Vol 18

Army Form C. 2118.

Copy 5

WAR DIARY
or
~~INTELLIGENCE SUMMARY.~~
(Erase heading not required.)

183 Machine Gun Company

Instructions regarding War Diaries and Intelligence Summaries are contained in F. S. Regs., Part II. and the Staff Manual respectively. Title pages will be prepared in manuscript.

Place	Date	Hour	Summary of Events and Information	Remarks and references to Appendices
FAMPOUX	1-11-17		Enemy Artillery – normal. TM's active at intervals. MG's normal. Our MG's carried out IF on usual tracks and communication trenches during the night. Aerial activity slight. Work on trenches continued.	E.H.
"	2-11-17		Enemy Artillery – more active than usual on support and back areas. TM's active all day on front and support lines. MG's normal. Our MG's carried out harrassing on communication trenches and tracks during the night. Work on Trenches, Dugouts, Emplacements etc.	E.H.
"	3-11-17		Enemy Artillery normal. Enemy TM's active from 10.0am to 10.45am and at 1.15pm and 5.0pm. MG's normal. Our MG's fired IF on CT's and tracks during the night.	5,500 Rds E.H.
"	4-11-17		Enemy Artillery quiet until 4.30pm when he retaliated heavily on Support & Reserve Lines till about 7.0pm. MG's normal. Our MG's carried out IF on usual tracks and CT's during the night; also fired in conjunction with raid by 47th Division on the Left. Total rounds fired 27,000.	E.H.

2353 Wt. W2544/1454 700,000 5/15 D. D. & L. A.D.S.S. Forms/C. 2118.

Instructions regarding War Diaries and Intelligence Summaries are contained in F. S. Regs., Part II. and the Staff Manual respectively. Title pages will be prepared in manuscript.

WAR DIARY

~~or~~

~~INTELLIGENCE SUMMARY.~~

(Erase heading not required.)

Army Form C. 2118.

183 Machine Gun Company

Place	Date	Hour	Summary of Events and Information	Remarks and references to Appendices
FAMPOUX	5-11-17		Enemy Artillery quiet. TM's normal. MG's normal. Our MG's left area shelled by Artillery under fire during the night. Usual harassing fire also carried out. 6,000 Rds.	[illegible]
"	6-11-17		Enemy Artillery below normal. TM's quiet. MG's normal. Our MG's in answer to Blue Lights fired on normal S.O.S line. Usual harassing fire carried out. 5,500 Rds.	[illegible]
"	7-11-17		Enemy Artillery – fairly active at intervals during the day. TM's normal. MG's quieter than usual. Our MG's carried out IF during the night. 5,250 Rds.	[illegible]
ARRAS	8-11-17		Company was relieved in the Line. CHEMICAL WORKS SECTOR by 184 M.G. Coy. Relief completed by 2.0. pm. Coy moved to Billets in LEVIS BARRACKS ARRAS.	[illegible]
"	9-11-17 10-11-17 11-11-17 12-11-17 13-11-17 14-11-17 15-11-17 16-11-17 17-11-17 18-11-17 19-11-17 20-11-17		General Training as per programme.	[illegible]

2353 Wt. W2544/1454 700,000 5/15 D. D. & L. A.D.S.S. Forms/C 2118.

Instructions regarding War Diaries and Intelligence Summaries are contained in F. S. Regs., Part II. and the Staff Manual respectively. Title pages will be prepared in manuscript.

WAR DIARY
or
~~INTELLIGENCE~~ SUMMARY.
(Erase heading not required.)

Army Form C. 2118.

183 Machine Gun Company

Place	Date	Hour	Summary of Events and Information	Remarks and references to Appendices
GREENLAND HILL	21-11-17		Coy relieved 182 MG Coy in the line, GREENLAND HILL SECTOR. Relief complete by 3 0pm without incident. Enemy Artillery active throughout the day. MG's active during the night. Our MG's fired on roads in conjunction with Operations of Brigade on Right, also carried out IF on tracks and CT's 13,000 Rds.	E.L.
" "	22-11-17	—	Enemy Artillery normal. T.M's quiet. MG's normal. Our MG's carried out IF at 3. 5am and during the night. 14,500 Rds.	E.L.
GREENLAND HILL	23-11-17		Enemy Artillery active during day, quiet at night. T.M's active at intervals. MG's normal. Our MG's fired on a party observed moving along WEED TRENCH and dispersed them. Also carried out Indirect Fire at night. 6000 Rds.	E.L.
" "	24-11-17		Enemy Artillery very active during the morning & afternoon. T.M's active on Front Line during morning and afternoon. MG's quiet. Our MG's carried out IF during the night at irregular intervals. 4,000 Rds.	E.L.

2353 Wt. W2544/1454 700,000 5/15 D. D. & L. A.D.S.S./Forms/C. 2118.

Army Form C. 2118.

WAR DIARY
or
INTELLIGENCE SUMMARY.

(Erase heading not required.)

183 Machine Gun Company

Place	Date	Hour	Summary of Events and Information	Remarks and references to Appendices
GREENLAND HILL	25.11.17		Enemy Artillery below normal. T.M's active all day on Front line. MG's normal. Our MG's carried out I.F. during night on enemy tracks and C.T's. 6,500 Rds.	[illegible]
— " —	26.11.17		Enemy Artillery active during the day and very active at night especially against Reserve and Support Lines. T.M's very active against Front & Support Lines. MG's quiet. Our MG's in addition to A.A firing carried out I.F during the night; total Rds. 4,000.	[illegible]
— " —	27.11.17		Enemy Artillery very active all day. MG's active during night. T.M's quiet. Our MG's carried out usual I.F. 8,000 Rds.	[illegible]
— " —	28.11.17		Coy was relieved in the Line by 2 Sections of 245th MG Coy. Relief complete by 11.10 pm. Coy moved to ARRAS. Billets in GALE COLLEGE.	[illegible]
"	29.11.17		General cleaning up. (Guns, Spare Parts, etc.) repacking Limbers and reorgizations.	[illegible]
"	30.11.17		Entrained at DAINVILLE at 7.30a and detrained at BAPAUME at 10.45a and proceeded to METZ TRESCAULT ROAD and bivouaced for the night	[illegible]

L. G. Ward Lt
OC 183 M.G. Coy

2353 Wt. W2544/1454 700,000 5/15 D. D. & L. A.D.S.S./Forms/C. 2118.

Vol 19

December 1917

War Diary

— of —

183rd Machine Gun Coy

Instructions regarding War Diaries and Intelligence Summaries are contained in F. S. Regs., Part II. and the Staff Manual respectively. Title pages will be prepared in manuscript.

WAR DIARY
or
INTELLIGENCE SUMMARY.
(Erase heading not required.)

Army Form C. 2118.

Place	Date	Hour	Summary of Events and Information	Remarks and references to Appendices
Metz.	1-12-17		Company marched from HAVRINCOURT. WOOD to billets in Metz. Sudden orders received 3 P.M. Company Proceeding to line, sixteen guns around LAVACQUERIE.	BL
	2-12-17		Huns raided trenches N. of LAVACQUERIE. six guns opened fire range 1200 yards. Bombing attack was also made by the enemy on our Brigade front and was only Partly driven off, Part of our trench system remained in enemies hands during the night. Four guns of No. 4 Section were relieved by two guns of No. 2. Section and took up Positions with the 2/7th Worcesters in the vicinity of Fern and Foster Trenches to Protect the right flank of the Brigade. On the left four guns were removed to Newport Trench The rest of the night was quiet:	BL
	3-12-17		Owing to enemy bombing Parties and to the failure of an attack by a battalion of 182 Brigade the situation at 6.30 AM was very obscure on left six guns being unprotected by infantry at 7.AM. the enemy commenced a heavy bombardment of our lines, at 7.50 A.M. it increased to a hurrican bombardment, at 8AM. enemy artillery lifted and they attacked, direct targets were engaged, but owing to the enemy^bombing^ Parties	BL

2353 Wt. W2544/1454 700,000 5/15 D. D. & L. A.D.S.S. Forms/C 2118.

Instructions regarding War Diaries and Intelligence Summaries are contained in F. S. Regs., Part II. and the Staff Manual respectively. Title pages will be prepared in manuscript.

WAR DIARY
or
INTELLIGENCE SUMMARY.

(Erase heading not required.)

Army Form C. 2118.

Place	Date	Hour	Summary of Events and Information	Remarks and references to Appendices
			Continued	
	3.12.17		getting round our flanks gun Positions became untenable and the guns put out of action, shortly after this the situation round LEVACQUERIE became obscure with the exception of the right flank which was defended by the 2/7th Worcesters and four Machine Guns, about 2 P.m. the situation cleared itself and the infantry then held the old British front line on the left and the centre with the exception of a small part of the LEVACQUERIE trench system know as the Corner Works. The rest of the day was quiet. Our Casualties were four officers and forty two other ranks and seven guns, during the night the 2/7th Worcesters withdrew to the Old British front line.	BM
	4.12.17		On the 4th quiet: Company reorganised into two Sections, attempt was made by the enemy to bomb our front trench which was unsuccessful. Four guns in Ferme Trench were moved back to support Trinity.	BM
	5.12.17		Enemy experimented during the morning with Artillery barrages no attack developed	BM

Instructions regarding War Diaries and Intelligence Summaries are contained in F. S. Regs., Part II. and the Staff Manual respectively. Title pages will be prepared in manuscript.

Army Form C. 2118.

WAR DIARY
or
INTELLIGENCE SUMMARY.
(Erase heading not required.)

Place	Date	Hour	Summary of Events and Information	Remarks and references to Appendices
			Continued	
	6.12.17		Company relieved by 184 Machine Gun Company, four guns were removed to billets in Metz remaining four guns to reserve in Lincoln Av.	[illegible]
	7.12.17		Four guns from Metz moved up into Reserve Line on Beauchamp Ridge	[illegible]
	8.12.17		Eight guns taken over by one Section and the remaining Section came back to billets in Equancourt.	[illegible]
	9.12.17		Quiet: Forty reinforcements other ranks arrived.	[illegible]
	10.12.17		Section in Equancourt moved up into Reserve Line.	[illegible]
	11.12.17		Quiet. Section organised from Reinforcements came up the line and took up barrage Positions in Frensham trench, the remaining eight guns from Reserve Line moved forward as follows: four to Barrage Positions, four to front line.	[illegible]
	12/12/17		Quiet.	
	13/12/17		Quiet, Machine Guns fired 8,000 rounds in conjunction with artillery throughout the night.	[illegible]
	14/12/17		Artillery normal, usual Machine Gun fire carried out.	[illegible]
	15/12/17		Ditto.	[illegible]

Army Form C. 2118.

Instructions regarding War Diaries and Intelligence Summaries are contained in F. S. Regs., Part II. and the Staff Manual respectively. Title pages will be prepared in manuscript.

WAR DIARY
or
INTELLIGENCE SUMMARY.
(Erase heading not required.)

Place	Date	Hour	Summary of Events and Information (Continued)	Remarks and references to Appendices
	16/12/17		Relieved by 184. Machine Gun Company, eight guns removed to billets in Metz, four guns moved to Reserve line and joined by other guns manned by remainder of reinforcements.	RL
	17/12/17		Quiet	RL
	18/12/17		Quiet	RL
	19/12/17		Normal	RL
	20/12/17		We relieved 182. Machine Gun Coy + 184 M.G.C in the line our positions being as follows, seven guns in barrage position, 4 guns in reserve line and five guns in front line.	RL
	21/12/17		Normal.	RL
	22/12/17		183. Machine Gun Coy relieved by 189. Machine Gun Coy: Company moved to billets in Metz.	RL
	23/12/17		Company marched to billets in Manancourt, transport remained Equancourt	RL
	24/12/17		Company left transport entrained Etricourt detrained Plateau Station marched Bray-sur-Somme to billets.	RL

2353 Wt. W2544/1454 700,000 5/15 D. D. & L. A.D.S.S. Forms/C. 2118.

Instructions regarding War Diaries and Intelligence Summaries are contained in F. S. Regs., Part II. and the Staff Manual respectively. Title pages will be prepared in manuscript.

WAR DIARY
or
INTELLIGENCE SUMMARY.
(Erase heading not required.)

Army Form C. 2118.

Place	Date	Hour	Summary of Events and Information	Remarks and references to Appendices
Continued				
	25/12/17		Owing to non arrival of lorries Christmas Festivities were Postponed	[illegible]
	26/12/17		General clean up of Stores etc.	[illegible]
	27/12/17		Reorganisation of Company.	[illegible]
	28/12/17		Transport inspected by B.O.C.	[illegible]
	29/12/17		Morning Work: Afternoon Christmas Feast.	[illegible]
	30/12/17		B.O.C inspects transport. Preparing for moving.	[illegible]
	31/12/17		Company marched to Marcelcave. via Harbonnières and Wiencourt arrived billets 12. P.m.	[illegible]

R. Leck Capt
CC 183 M.G.C.
31-12-17

Vol 20

January 1918

War Diary

~ of ~

183rd Machine Gun Coy

Army Form C. 2118.

WAR DIARY
or
~~INTELLIGENCE SUMMARY.~~
(Erase heading not required.)

Instructions regarding War Diaries and Intelligence Summaries are contained in F. S. Regs., Part II. and the Staff Manual respectively. Title pages will be prepared in manuscript.

VOLUME
JANUARY 1918.

183 MACHINE GUN COY

Place	Date	Hour	Summary of Events and Information	Remarks and references to Appendices
MARCELCAVE Ref. Sheet AMIENS.	1st		Coy in billets at MARCELCAVE, marched in previous afternoon. RGY	
	2nd		Commenced training according to Schedule. 2 OR proceeded to UK on leave. RGY	APPENDIX I & II Training Programme.
	3rd		Five NCO's & men found dead & two NCO's seriously ill with coal gas poisoning from a brazier in Company Orderly room. Men buried on the 5th at CERISY GAILLY Franco British cemetery. Continued Company training. RGY	
	4th		Training according to programme. 2/Lt MONTGOMERY proceeded to join M.G. anti aircraft & M.G. course at French Army. Court of Enquiry held with reference to the casualties caused by coal gas poisoning on the 3rd. RGY	
	5th		Information received that CAPT. D.H. LECK. O.C has been awarded the M.C. Training continued. RGY	
	6th		Coy. prepares to move to the NESLE area. LIEUT E.G. WARDROP & 2 OR proceed to join G.H.Q. Small arms School. CAMIERS. Machine Gun Course. RGY	
ROIGLISE Ref. Sheet 66D 1:40.000	7th		Company moved from MARCELCAVE to ROIGLISE by march route via ROYE. Roads very bad & thickly covered with snow, but able to report clear "Falling Out" sheet. RGY	
	8th		Day spent in rest & preparing to move to forward area. RGY	
FALVY Ref. Sheet 66D.	9th		Company marched to FALVY in reserve to 61st Division. Comfortable billets. Weather still frosty. RGY	

2353 Wt. W2544/1454 700,000 5/15 D. D. & L. A.D.S.S. Forms/C 2118.

Army Form

Instructions regarding War Diaries and Intelligence Summaries are contained in F. S. Regs., Part II. and the Staff Manual respectively. Title pages will be prepared in manuscript.

WAR DIARY
or
~~INTELLIGENCE SUMMARY~~.
(Erase heading not required.)

JANUARY 1918. 183. MACHINE GUN Coy.

Place	Date	Hour	Summary of Events and Information	Remarks and references to Appendices
Ref. Sheet 66D 1:40,000 FALVY	10th		Frosty weather still continues, Company carry out advanced training as per programme. R.G.F. ~~LIEUT~~	
	11th		Company Training continued. ~~RGF~~ 1OR to U.K. on leave RGF	
	12th		Company Training continued. RGF	
	13th		Company Training continued RGF	
	14th		Company Training continued. LIEUT FRYER returned from leave to U.K. RGF	
Ref Sheet 62C S.E. 1:20,000	15th		Company marched from FALVY to BEAUVOIS preparatory to relieving 182 Brigade in the line. 1OR. returned from leave. RGF.	
	16th		Weather changed, rained most of the day making training difficult. RGF	
	17th	8.30am	Coy marched to UGNY-l'EQUIPÉE for Generals inspection & presentation of decorations. on arrival parade postponed.	
		10.am	Company prepared Guns & equipment ready for relief of 182 Brigade on 18th RGF O.C. + Gun team commanders proceed to line for reconnaissance of Sector.	
	18th		Company marched to UGNY-l'EQUIPÉE & formed part of General parade for presentation of decorations by G.O.C. Division. Company recipients were 6405 C.S.M. Amos S. D.C.M. 28522 Sergt Lee, A. D.C.M. 36784. Sgt Garbett J. M.M. 23358. L/Cpl McKay J. M.M. 1OR returned from leave. 1OR evacuated to C.C.S. sick	

2353 Wt. W2544/1454 700,000 5/15 D. D. & L. A.D.S.S. Forms/C 2118.

Instructions regarding War Diaries and Intelligence Summaries are contained in F. S. Regs., Part II. and the Staff Manual respectively. Title pages will be prepared in manuscript.

Army Form

WAR DIARY
or
INTELLIGENCE SUMMARY.
(Erase heading not required.)

JANUARY 1918. 183. MACHINE GUN Coy.

Place	Date	Hour	Summary of Events and Information	Remarks and references to Appendices
Ref Sheet 62CSE 1:20,000	18th	Contd.	8 OR reported from M.G.C. Base as reinforcements. Company moved	
		5pm	off at dusk & relieved 182 MACHINE GUN Coy in Right Brigade Sector of	
S.10.c.30.95.			61st Div. front, St QUENTIN. whole front extremely quiet, relief successfully completed by 10pm. accomodation in the line good. 16 Guns in position. Company Headquarters S.10.c.30.95. owing to shortage of officers a Sergt is in charge of one Section. RPL	
	19th		Front continues very quiet, our aircraft very active & heavily engaged by enemy AA Guns & M.G's. Our M.G's fired occasional bursts during the night. active patrolling along Brigade front. our wire in fairly good condition. 1 OR proceeded on leave to U.K. RPL	
	20th		Enemy artillery a little more active, shelling roads & tracks during the morning. our artillery carried out registration. Aerial activity above normal. one Enemy machine observed about 11.45 am dropping lights behind our line for artillery registration. 2 of our machines dropped bombs on St QUENTIN, 1 OR returned from leave. RPL	
			267 MACHINE GUN Coy joined the 61st Div. as Divisional Machine Gun Coy.	

2353 Wt. W2544/1454 700,000 5/15 D. D. & L. A.D.S.S. Forms/C. 2118.

Instructions regarding War Diaries and Intelligence Summaries are contained in F. S. Regs., Part II. and the Staff Manual respectively. Title pages will be prepared in manuscript.

Army Form C. 2

WAR DIARY
or
INTELLIGENCE SUMMARY.
(*Erase heading not required.*)

JANUARY 1918 — 183 MACHINE GUN COY.

Place	Date	Hour	Summary of Events and Information	Remarks and references to Appendices
Ref Sheet 62C.S.E. 1:20.000 S10.c.30.95.	21st		Rain during morning. received orders that all units should be specially vigilant at 4am. but day passed without any exceptional incident. between 3.45 – 4.30pm Enemy sent up various coloured very lights and rockets along the whole of the Divisional front. it is assumed he was trying to discover our SOS signal. as no action took place. Enemy artillery moderately active during day, night very quiet. Orders received that Enemy may project gas on this front. all ranks warned & necessary precautions taken. RJ4.	
	22nd		Quiet day. very little artillery activity. Our Machine Guns fired occasional bursts during the night. Enemy Machine Guns not so active as usual. Weather fair. RJ4.	
	23rd		Another quiet and uneventful day, our Artillery shelled Enemy lines between 11.50am & 2.30pm. One of our Machine Guns fired on Enemy movement in ROCOURT SALIENT at 2.30pm. Enemy Artillery & MG's below normal. 2/LT's FARROW & 2/LT ASPLAND from Base as reinforcements RJ4	

Army Form C. 2118.

Instructions regarding War Diaries and Intelligence Summaries are contained in F. S. Regs., Part II. and the Staff Manual respectively. Title pages will be prepared in manuscript.

WAR DIARY
or
~~INTELLIGENCE SUMMARY.~~
(Erase heading not required.)

JANUARY 1918. 183. MACHINE GUN Coy

Place	Date	Hour	Summary of Events and Information	Remarks and references to Appendices
S.10.c.30.95	24th		Quiet along Divisional front. Enemy made silent raid on one of our advanced infantry posts at about 6 am, 2 of our infantry men are missing. One N.C.O. left for CAMIERS for dispatch to England to attend special Course at GRANTHAM. One O.R. admitted to hospital sick. LIEUT E WARDROP appointed 2nd in command of this Company. RPL	
	25th		Both our own & enemy artillery showed greater activity & a considerable increase was observed in Enemy aerial work about 10 am. 5 E.A. crossed our lines to N.W. & remained over dropping bombs on back areas for about 2 hours. RPL	
	26th		Very misty, consequently artillery inactive, & no intelligence was obtained by observation of movement. During the night our Machine Guns fired occasional bursts & worked on the improvement of emplacements & trenches. RPL	
	27th		Again misty and only a few shells fired by enemy during the day, our artillery remained quiet. Machine Guns both enemy's & ours were active during night. 2/Lt MONTGOMERY	

2353 Wt. W2544/1454 700,000 5/15 D. D. & L. A.D.S.S. Forms/C. 2118.

Instructions regarding War Diaries and Intelligence Summaries are contained in F. S. Regs., Part II. and the Staff Manual respectively. Title pages will be prepared in manuscript.

WAR DIARY
or
~~INTELLIGENCE SUMMARY~~.
(Erase heading not required.)

Army Form C. 2118.

JANUARY 1918 — 183 MACHINE GUN COY

Place	Date	Hour	Summary of Events and Information	Remarks and references to Appendices
S.10c.30.95.	27th		& 1 OR returned from AA course with French army. One OR admitted to Hospital. One Officer & 12 men from Divisional Machine Gun Coy were attached to this Coy for 2 days instruction in the line. RLG	
	28th		Weather fine, & clear. Artillery showed considerable activity. Our artillery shelled ST QUENTIN during morning. During the night our Machine Guns fired on N31C.Y.8. & on ROCOURT SALIENT. Work on improvement of Gun positions carried out. RLG	
	29th		Enemy & own aircraft exceptionally active. EA's continually over our lines, several bombs being dropped & at night several EA crossed our lines & bombed back areas. Own machines flew over Enemy lines & ~~[illegible]~~ engaged several ground targets with M.G. fire, drawing heavy AA fire. RLG	
	30th		Quiet day on whole front. Considerable aerial activity both by day & night. Our wire was cut by enemy shell fire in	

Army Form C. 2118.

WAR DIARY
or
~~INTELLIGENCE SUMMARY.~~

Instructions regarding War Diaries and Intelligence Summaries are contained in F. S. Regs., Part II. and the Staff Manual respectively. Title pages will be prepared in manuscript.

JANUARY 1918 (*Erase heading not required.*) 183 MACHINE GUN Coy

Place	Date	Hour	Summary of Events and Information	Remarks and references to Appendices
Sheet 62 B SW				
S10.c.30.95	30th		front of FAYET our Machine guns were laid on point in front of gaps but Enemy took no action. Our MG's fired bursts throughout night & engaged hostile aeroplanes during day. 2 new gun positions occupied in line of redoubts at S14.b.40.60. Several new positions have been reconnoitred for new machine gun defense scheme. RJ	
	31st		Weather misty making observation impossible. Artillery activity nil. Machine guns fired occasional bursts. Two of our forward Machine guns withdrawn to position in rear at S14.a.30.60. 2/Lt WICKS to UK on leave. RJ	

[signature]
OC 183 MGC

No. 183 MACHINE GUN COMPANY. No. 9 1 18 Date

2353 Wt. W2544/1454 700,000 5/15 D. D. & L. A.D.S.S. Forms/C 2118.

APPENDIX I

183 MACHINE GUN COMPANY.

TRAINING PROGRAMME FROM 16TH JANUARY, 1918.

PLACE	HOURS.	DESCRIPTION OF TRAINING.	REMARKS.
		FIRST DAY – JAN. 16TH	
TRAINING AREA:	9am. to 10am.	Physical Drill and Squad Drill.	O.C.'s PARADE DAILY.
	10am " 11am.	Mechanism and Belt Filling.	
	11am " 12noon.	Stoppages.	
	12noon " 12.30pm.	Gas Drill.	
	12.30pm " 1pm.	Anti-Aircraft Instruction and Use of A.A. Sights.	
	2pm " 4pm.	Recreation.	
		SECOND DAY – JAN. 17TH	
	9am. to 11am.	Range for Nos 1 & 2 Sections. Nos. 3 & 4 Sections: Stripping; Mechanism. Stoppages.	
"	11am " 1pm.	Range for Nos. 3 & 4 Sections. Nos. 1 & 2 Sections: Stripping; Mechanism. Stoppages.	
	2pm " 4pm.	Recreation.	
	5pm " 6pm.	Lecture: Care of Feet.	

O.C. 183 M.G. Coy.

APPENDIX II

183 MACHINE GUN COMPANY

TRAINING PROGRAMME FROM January 2nd 1918

PLACE	HOURS	DESCRIPTION OF TRAINING.	REMARKS.
		FIRST DAY – Jan. 2.	
TRAINING AREA	9·0 am to 10·0 am	Physical Drill and Squad Drill	
	10·0 am – 11·0 am	Mechanism	
	11·0 am – 12 noon	Stoppages	C O's PARADE
	12·0 noon – 1·0 pm	Belt Filling	
	2·0 pm – 4·0 pm	Recreation	DAILY
	5·0 pm – 6·0 pm	Lecture: Range Discipline: Self Inflicted Wounds, Points B D A Firing	
		SECOND DAY – Jan 3	
	9·0 am to 11·0 am	Range for Nos 1 and 2 Sections 3 and 4 Sections Stripping Mechanism	
	11·0 am – 1·0 pm	Range for Nos 3 and 4 Sections 1 and 2 Sections Stripping Mechanism	
	2·0 pm – 4·0 pm	Recreation	
	5·0 pm – 6·0 pm	Lecture: Indirect Fire Use of Clinometer	
		THIRD DAY – Jan. 4	
	9·0 am to 10·0 am	Physical Drill and Squad Drill	
	10·0 am – 11·0 am	Mechanism	
	11·0 am – 12·0 noon	Gun Drill	
	12·0 noon – 1·0 pm	Stoppages	
	2·0 pm – 4·0 pm	Recreation	
	5·0 pm – 6·0 pm	Lecture: Indirect Fire Use of Clinometer	

PLACE	HOURS	DESCRIPTION OF TRAINING	REMARKS
TRAINING AREA		FOURTH DAY – Jan 5.	O.C.s PARADE DAILY
	9.0 am to 11.0 am	Range for 1 and 2 Sections firing Stoppages with & without Respirators 3 and 4 Sections Stoppages and Mechanism	
	11.0 am – 1.0 pm	Range for 3 and 4 Sections firing Stoppages with and without Respirators	
	11.0 am – 1.0 pm	1 and 2 Sections Stoppages also Mechanism	
	2.0 pm – 4.0 pm	Recreation	
	5.0 pm – 6.0 pm	Lecture Compass Map Reading	
		FIFTH DAY – ~~Jan 6th~~	
	9.0 am – 10.0 am	Physical Drill and Squad Drill	
	10.0 am – 11.0 am	Stoppages	
	11.0 am – 12 noon	Gun Drill	
	12 noon – 1.0 pm	Gas Drill	
	2.0 pm – 4.0 pm	Recreation	
	5.0 pm – 6.0 pm	Lecture – Compass – Map Reading	
		SIXTH DAY	
	9.0 am to 11.0 am	Range for 1 and 2 Sections. Combined Sights. Traversing. Vert. Searching, Adv Work 3 and 4 Sections. Stripping and Stoppages	
	11.0 am – 1.0 pm	Range for 3 & 4 Sections. Combined Sights Vert Searching. Advanced Work 1 and 2 Sections Stripping and Stoppages.	
	2.0 pm – 4.0 pm	Recreation	
	5.0 pm – 6.0 pm	Lecture: Barrage Fire	
		SEVENTH DAY	
	9.0 am to 10.0 am	Physical Drill	
	10.0 am – 11.0 am	Cleaning Guns and Stores	
	11.0 am – 1.0 pm	Examination of Belts and Packing of Limbers	
	2.0 pm – 4.0 pm	Recreation	
	5.0 pm – 6.0 pm	Lecture – Methods of Relief	

WAR DIARY
or
INTELLIGENCE SUMMARY.

Instructions regarding War Diaries and Intelligence Summaries are contained in F. S. Regs., Part II. and the Staff Manual respectively. Title pages will be prepared in manuscript.

FEBRUARY 1918. (Erase heading not required.) 183 MACHINE GUN COY

Place	Date	Hour	Summary of Events and Information	Remarks and references to Appendices
R/Sheet 62B S.W. 1:20,000 S10C 30.95.	1st		Weather Misty no artillery activity. Hostile Machine Gun battery of 6 or 8 Guns fired at our lines rapid for 10 mins at 7.30 pm & for 8 mins at 8.15 pm. Between 4 pm & 5 pm a test was carried out with one of the Company's Machine Guns to try what effect firing several thousand rounds without the check lever had on the gun, the result was satisfactory. 7000 Rounds expended during the night on enemy tracks, roads etc. Two Lewis Guns & teams attached to us from the Pioneer Battalion & placed in vacated Vickers Gun positions. 1 OR to Hospital sick. R.P.S.	
	2nd		CO & Section Officers of 184 Machine Gun Coy reconnoitered our Sector preparatory to relief. Test firing without check lever continued; recommended that check lever & bracket be abolished. Artillery again quiet but M.G's showed increased activity. 2 OR admitted to Hospital sick. R.P.S.	
	3rd		Our Artillery fairly active. Enemy back areas, ROCOURT SALIENT & CEPY FARM received considerable attention. Our Aircraft continually crossed Enemy lines & several bombs were dropped. Machine Guns were normal	

contd.

2353 Wt. W2544/1454 700,000 5/15 D. D. & L. A.D.S.S. Forms/C 2118.

Army Form C. 2118.

Instructions regarding War Diaries and Intelligence Summaries are contained in F. S. Regs., Part II. and the Staff Manual respectively. Title pages will be prepared in manuscript.

WAR DIARY
or
INTELLIGENCE SUMMARY.
(Erase heading not required.)

FEBRUARY 1918 — 183 MACHINE GUN COY

Place	Date	Hour	Summary of Events and Information	Remarks and references to Appendices
Ref Sheet FRANCE. ST. QUENTIN 1:100.000 300x S of X in VAUX.	3rd	5pm	183 Infantry Brigade relieved by the 184 Infantry Brigade. Relief of this Company completed successfully by 8.30pm. Company moved to billets in VAUX & became part of Reserve Brigade to 61st Division with orders to proceed to ATTILLY on receipt of wire "man battle Stations". RJL	APPENDIX "Programme of Training"
	4th		Day spent in cleaning & overhauling Gun Equipment & personal Equipment Baths at ETTREILLERS. 2 Gun teams & one officer on AA duty at BEAUVOIS. RJL	
	5th		Training carried out as per programme APPENDIX I. 2/Lt RICHARDS admitted to Field Ambulance sick. 2 OR reinforcements reported from A.H.T.D. RJL	
	6th		O.C. & Section Officers reconnoitered left Brigade Sector. Training carried out. 2 OR's to hospital sick. LIEUT WARDROP + 2 OR's returned from months Course at G.H.Q. Small Arms School CAMIERS. RJL	
	7th		Training continued. 1 OR from Hospital RJL	
	8th		Training Continued. RJL	
	9th		2/Lt RICHARDS transferred to C.C.S. Training continued. RJL	
	10th		Church Parades at VAUX. 1 O.R. to Hospital Sick. 1 NCO to Course of P.T. & BF at ST. POL. Nos 1 of each Gun & runners went into the line in	

Instructions regarding War Diaries and Intelligence Summaries are contained in F. S. Regs., Part II. and the Staff Manual respectively. Title pages will be prepared in manuscript.

WAR DIARY
or
INTELLIGENCE SUMMARY.
(Erase heading not required.)

Army Form C. 2118.

FEBRUARY 1918 — 183 MACHINE GUN COY

Place	Date	Hour	Summary of Events and Information	Remarks and references to Appendices
VAUX	10th		left Sector as advance party to take over gun positions etc. RJL	
Ref Sheet 62BSW 1:20000 H24a 6.8 FRESNOY	11th		Preparing guns & packing limbers etc for the line. 183 M.G. Coy relieved 182 M.G. Coy in the left Sector, relief successfully completed 8.30pm. 1OR reported from hospital. Between 9pm & 11pm hostile aeroplanes were heard over our lines. RJL	
	12th	12.15 am	Sector quiet, very little artillery or machine gun activity. Cavalry Division on left carried out a successful raid on M3.abc. under cover of Artillery & Machine Gun barrage. Enemy party raided one of our advanced posts one of the raiders was killed & one of our men and a Lewis Gun missing. 2OR reported from leave to UK. RJL	
	13th		Weather bad. Misty & wet. Activity nil. Machine guns fired occasional bursts throughout the night. RJL	
	14th		Weather misty. Artillery & M.G's quiet. 1.OR to hospital sick. RJL	
	15th		Weather fine & clear. Our 18pdrs fired 100 rounds in registration. Our aircraft active. M.G's fired bursts of fire during night on Enemy lines. E.A. dropped bombs on HOLNON during the evening. One OR to UK on leave. RJL	

2353 Wt. W2544/1454 700,000 5/15 D. D. & L. A.D.S.S. Forms/C. 2118.

Instructions regarding War Diaries and Intelligence Summaries are contained in F. S. Regs., Part II. and the Staff Manual respectively. Title pages will be prepared in manuscript.

WAR DIARY
or
INTELLIGENCE SUMMARY.
(Erase heading not required.)

Army Form C. 2118.

FEBRUARY 1918 — 183 MACHINE GUN Coy.

Place	Date	Hour	Summary of Events and Information	Remarks and references to Appendices
FRESNOY	16th		Considerable general activity. at 12.30pm one of our Bristol Fighting aeroplanes was brought down in flames by EA. Capt LECK to UK on 1 months special leave. LIEUT WARDROP assumes command of Company LIEUT RG. FRYER a/Second in Command. RGF	
	17th		Sector fairly quiet. our artillery registered FRESNOY CEMETERY during the afternoon. LT. FRYER proceeded to HAM to attend 3 day Corps Commanders conference on Training & Work. 20 OR'S attached from Infantry Batts pending transfer. 2 Lewis Gun teams relieved. RGF	
	18th		Our artillery fired about 150 Rounds on enemy's support line M12c 3.3 & THORIGNY. aircraft own & Enemy very active. bombs dropped behind enemy lines. 2 OR'S from hospital. one OR to hospital with accidental revolver shot wound in foot. RGF	
	19th		Warning order received stating that Coy would have guns relieved by Canadian Cavalry Brigade on night 21/22 & notes on readjustment of Sector. Considerable aircraft activity. our MG's expended 500 rounds on EA. RGF	

2353 Wt. W2544/1454 700,000 5/15 D. D. & L. A.D.S.S. Forms/C 2118.

Army Form C. 2118.

WAR DIARY
or
INTELLIGENCE SUMMARY.
(*Erase heading not required.*)

Instructions regarding War Diaries and Intelligence Summaries are contained in F. S. Regs., Part II. and the Staff Manual respectively. Title pages will be prepared in manuscript.

FEBRUARY 1918 — 183 Machine Gun Coy.

Place	Date	Hour	Summary of Events and Information	Remarks and references to Appendices
FRESNOY	20th		Artillery & MG's normal except between midnight & 2am when there was a bombardment on the left Sector. 2/LT STEEL appointed Transport Officer to 61st Div. Machine from Battalion. one OR from Hospital. LIEUT R.G.FRYER returns from Conference at HAM. RGF	
	21st		Considerable increase in Artillery activity. Aircraft active & continually engaged by Enemy AA guns. our MG's fired during the day at EA flying low. RGF.	
	22nd		Weather dull & misty, activity below normal. 2/Lt WICKS returned from leave to UK. RGF	
	23rd		Quiet during day. One EA which crossed our lines appeared to be a new type, a two seater tractor biplane tail shaped like armstrong Whitworth. upper plane staggered back & over hung, one pair of struts on each wing set at an angle. About 9.30pm owing to an	
		9.30	encounter in front of GRICOURT between one of our fighting patrols & an enemy bombing party, enemy put down a barrage which	

2353 Wt. W2544/1454 700,000 5/15 D. D. & L. A.D.S.S. Forms/C 2118.

Army Form C. 2118.

Instructions regarding War Diaries and Intelligence Summaries are contained in F. S. Regs., Part II. and the Staff Manual respectively. Title pages will be prepared in manuscript.

WAR DIARY
or
INTELLIGENCE SUMMARY.
(Erase heading not required.)

FEBRUARY 1918 — 183 MACHINE GUN COY

Place	Date	Hour	Summary of Events and Information	Remarks and references to Appendices
FRESNOY	23rd		was preceded by red & green lights sent up by the enemy, our artillery replied by putting down an intense barrage on the Enemy front line for 45 mins. 3 of our forward M.G's mistook the red lights for our SOS signal & opened rapid fire on SOS lines, one gun being slightly damaged by fragment of shell. R.G.	
	24th		Own & Enemy planes & artillery active, some of our machines engaging ground targets with M.G. A bombing plane, believed to be one of our own was brought down at midnight by gun fire on right. R.G.	
	25th		Considerable Artillery activity on both sides, M.G's active during night especially between 9.30 & 10pm. Our planes dropped several bombs behind enemy lines in the evening. 2 O.R's to Water duty Course at GERMAINE. R.G.	
	26th		Normal activity during day, but between midnight & 12.30 am our Artillery put down barrage in reply to Enemy bombardment on left Sector. Our M.G's active against E.A. during day. 1 O.R to hospital. 1 O.R from hospital. R.G.	

2353 Wt. W2544/1454 700,000 5/15 D. D. & L. A.D.S.S. Forms/C. 2118.

Instructions regarding War Diaries and Intelligence Summaries are contained in F. S. Regs., Part II. and the Staff Manual respectively. Title pages will be prepared in manuscript.

Army Form C. 2118.

WAR DIARY
or
INTELLIGENCE SUMMARY.

FEBRUARY 1918 *(Erase heading not required.)* 183 MACHINE GUN COY

Place	Date	Hour	Summary of Events and Information	Remarks and references to Appendices
FRESNOY	27th		Company relieved by 184 Machine Gun Coy. two sections & Headquarters to VAUX & 2 Sections in Reserve to battle Zone in ATTILLY, relief complete at 9 pm without incident. all quiet on battle front during day & to time of relief. 2 OR's to hospital. RJL	
VAUX	28th		Cleaning up gun kit etc. packing limbers ready to move. 2/Lt W. McDOUGALL & 1 OR reinforcements from Base. RJL	

RJ Fryer Lieut
for OC 183 Machine Gun Coy

No. 183
MACHINE GUN
COMPANY.
No. 27
Date 28/2/18

2353 Wt. W2544/1454 700,000 5/15 D. D. & L. A.D.S.S. Forms/C. 2118.

61ST DIVISION
183RD INFY BDE

183RD MACHINE GUN COY.

JUN 1916-FEB 1918

Instructions regarding War Diaries and Intelligence Summaries are contained in F. S. Regs., Part II. and the Staff Manual respectively. Title Pages will be prepared in manuscript.

June '16
Feb '18

WAR DIARY
or
~~INTELLIGENCE SUMMARY~~

(Erase heading not required.)

183 M. G. Coy.
June 1916
Vol 1

Army Form C. 2118. 61

Place	Date	Hour	Summary of Events and Information	Remarks and references to Appendices
Le Havre	17.6.16	11.0am	Transport arrived & disembarkation commenced. Arrived in rest	CW
		4.30pm	Camp No 1 at about 4.30pm. Kit inspection carried out	CW
"	18.6.16		Stores to complete establishment were drawn as far as possible	CW
		11.30am	Received orders to entrain, half a company with each of two specified trainloads	CW
		11.39pm	After completing entrainment of 1st half company left Le Havre	CW
	19.6.16	3.0am	" " 2nd " "	CW
[illegible]		1.30pm	Arrived La Gorgue (1st ½ Coy) with 182 Coy train	CW
		11.30pm	After detraining arrived in Laventie. Billets at Chateau.	CW
	20.6.16	2.30am	2nd ½ Coy arrived La Gorgue with 184 Coy train	CW
		11.30am	" " " in billets.	CW
			The day was spent in general cleaning up	CW
Laventie	21.6.16	10.0am	Inspection by Major General Colin Mackenzie C.B. G.O.C. 61st Division.	CW
		2.0pm to 4.0pm	Drill & instruction.	CW
"	22.6.16		"	
			Orders received to move to Fort du Rom. Attached to 182 Bde, Laventie, for operations	CW
	23.6.16	12.30pm	Transport & details to Laventie remaining.	CW
		4.30pm	arrived at Fort du Rom	CW
Fort du Rom	24.6.16	9.0am	Inspected the positions occupied by 105 M. G. Coy. & all officers. Arrangements were made for two sections to move up to the front line for instruction. Nos 1 & 2 sections moved up between 3.0 & 5.0pm.	CW

C W Walker

2449 Wt. W14957/M90 750,000 1/16 J.B.C. & A. Forms/C.2118/12.

www.ingramcontent.com/pod-product-compliance
Lightning Source LLC
Chambersburg PA
CBHW081403160426
43193CB00013B/2092
* 9 7 8 1 4 7 4 5 3 3 2 6 3 *